BEFORE

MY HEART

STOPS

BEFORE

MY HEART

STOPS

a memoir

PAUL CARDALL

SHADOW
MOUNTAIN

For Eden and Lynnette
Families are forever

Visit us at ShadowMountain.com

Library of Congress Cataloging-in-Publication Data
Cardall, Paul.
  Before my heart stops : a memoir / Paul Cardall.
  p. cm.
  Includes bibliographical references and index.
  Summary: Born with a severe congenital heart defect, talented musician Paul Cardall has struggled all his life. Through engaging blogs and flashbacks, he relates his experiences of waiting for his heart transplant.
  ISBN 978-1-60641-818-5 (hardbound : alk. paper)
  1. Cardall, Paul. 2. Pianists—United States—Biography. 3. Heart—Transplantation—Patients—Utah. 4. Mormons—Biography. I. Title.
  ML417.C28A3 2010
  786.2092—dc22
  [B]   2010019692

Printed in the United States of America
Publishers Printing

10 9 8 7 6 5 4 3 2

CONTENTS

ACKNOWLEDGMENTS

*M*ost people write about their experience after it is over. For me, writing my story as I experienced the struggles of severe heart failure became my therapy and daily affirmation as I waited for a life-or-death heart transplant procedure.

This book would not have been possible without the love, support, and friendship of my beautiful wife, Lynnette, and my sweet daughter, Eden, who together have been my muses. Thoughts of leaving them behind inspired me to write my feelings and observations down as though it might be my last chance in this life to tell them how much I love them.

I was born to remarkable parents, Duane and Margaret Cardall, and surrounded by wonderful siblings who never allowed my chronic illness to keep me from doing the things I wanted to do. Constantly by my bedside offering prayers of faith, they implanted in my heart seeds of optimism and trust in a loving God. My father Duane Cardall, a gifted journalist, encouraged me to share my story with others, and I love him for inspiring me to write.

People are brought into our lives for a reason. My adult congenital cardiologist, Angela T. Yetman, who put me on a path for a second chance at life, has become like a sister to me. After carefully reviewing this book, she's made wonderful suggestions and edits that I believe have improved a general understanding of my faith and medical condition.

I'm grateful to Donald M. Doty, MD, a gifted cardiovascular thoracic surgeon who has performed thousands of miraculous surgeries—including my early procedures—for his input in helping me explain my surgical procedures in a way that would be helpful to the reader.

Thanks also to my wonderful friends at Shadow Mountain Publishing: to Chris Schoebinger for believing in this project so strongly and pushing it forward with such passion; to Leslie Stitt, my wonderful editor, for your hard work and many hours helping me say the things of my heart with much greater understanding; to Rachael Ward, my typesetter; to Richard Erickson and Sheryl Dickert Smith, my design team, who brought clarity and vision to this book; and to Bob Ahlander and my friends at Shadow Mountain Music for supporting my decision to write a book and explore and desire another talent from our Heavenly Father. A special thank you to Linda Prince, who helped me organize and pre-edit my story and message.

Finally, to the vast community of neighbors, friends, and those who followed my journey on my blog: http://www.living foreden.com—you have made this possible.

FOREWORD

There must be a God. How else can you explain all that is beautiful in the world?"

These words were spoken to me long ago, and through the years they have given me pause. They resonated with me, yet I was often quick to dismiss them, falling back on a belief in a lack of belief.

This story is about a journey—the journey of a man in search of a heart. Along the way, his path intersected with that of many others, and many lives were enriched. One of these was mine. During this yearlong journey, I came to see all that is beautiful in the world.

Medicine is an odd career. It takes one down a path filled with death and suffering—certainly not what one would consciously choose to focus on. Rarely does a physician see or fully realize the fruits of his or her labor. The healed move on. They do not linger in the hospital. It is the sick and dying that are ever-present day after day. Hospitalized children are not filled with that natural joy that one sees in the outside world. The parents of these children are filled with guilt, worry, and dread. It is their suffering over lost potential and an unknown future that one sees.

The field of pediatric cardiovascular surgery has evolved to the point that for most infants born with heart defects, some form of surgery can be performed so that they may live to see another day. However, such surgery is often not curative. Plumbing is rerouted, holes are closed or created, and blood diverted, offering short-term answers. There will be more surgeries, months spent in the hospital, physical restrictions, and cognitive impairment.

This harsh reality weighs heavily on many of us, leading us to ask many more questions and to reflect on the pain of life lost. Is it harder to have your child die at ten days of age or at ten years of age? Is it easier to let a child die, or to live and face innumerable surgeries, all the while knowing that he or she will probably not live to adulthood? Those patients who do reach adulthood will face seemingly endless uncertainties: how will they qualify for the health insurance they desperately need? should they marry and have children knowing that they probably won't see their children grow up? As physicians, should we be brutally honest and paint this grave picture, or should we offer support and hope to the parents and then to the patients themselves? The former would instill worry and fear; the latter would conceal the truth. Is it our ethical obligation to be positive or to be completely forthright? These are the questions that weighed heavily on my mind.

A MOST FORTUNATE INTERSECTION

I was on my path. Paul was on his. In early summer 2008, the two intersected.

I do not think patients fully realize how they shape our lives. It only takes a moment for a life to change, to be enriched. But how could this man—this pale, quiet, edematous man on more medications than one could count on both hands—have the emotional and physical power to initiate such a change?

This patient, Paul Cardall, would forever change my life, would reinvigorate me and bring me life. Paul had end-stage heart failure. We talked about options. There were no easy options. He could choose to live or choose to die. The latter would be easier. He chose life, not passively, but vigorously, with the kind of energy that left me asking what I had been doing with my own life. I don't think he was afraid to die. He just needed to live. He had unfinished business. He was not beholden to any physical thing of this world. Rather, he embraced everything of this world—embraced it as part of God's glory, realizing the beauty that surrounded him every day. He knew he still had work here to do.

Over the ensuing months, when I was heavy of heart, knowing that he would not likely live, I was always uplifted by his spirit. In our weekly visits, we talked medicine, and we talked religion. I altered his medications and prescribed new therapies. He altered my outlook on life, and prescribed readings from different religious works. I acquired an optimism and faith that I had never known. He grew physically weaker but remained spiritually strong. We grew as a team—a team devoted to a cause. Somehow, we were going to beat the odds. With a combination of faith in something much greater than ourselves, and the resources to build the best medical team possible, we would arrange for the successful heart transplant of a thirty-six-year-old gentleman with a failing heart. Having survived five previous cardiac surgeries, and with liver damage and gastrointestinal dysfunction, Paul was a poor candidate for a heart transplant. It would be technically difficult and possibly fatal. Despite the odds, we remained committed to the cause, all the while joking about the book he would write at the end of this stage of the journey. This is his story.

ANGELA T. YETMAN, MD
Director, Adult Congenital Heart Disease Program
Primary Children's Medical Center
Intermountain Medical Center
University of Utah Medical Center

INTRODUCTION

*W*hen I was ten years old, a young boy in our neighborhood had cancer. Andrew was bald, and he looked strange to me. I thought about Andrew a great deal. I loved his family and practically idolized one of his older brothers, who led most of our night-game activities. In the early evenings, Andrew's mother and father walked around the block with their little boy in a stroller.

Andrew didn't survive the cancer. In the middle of the night following the viewing at the mortuary, I started crying, haunted at the thought of Andrew lying in a casket. I left the basement bedroom I shared with my younger brothers and headed toward my parents' room. My father had heard me crying, and he met me at the bottom of the basement stairs. With great concern, he asked me what was wrong. I told him that it hurt so much and that I didn't understand why Andrew had to die. Dad just held me and told me it would be okay—that Andrew was with Heavenly Father now.

Every time I rode by Andrew's home delivering news-papers, I thought about how he had been lying on the couch with a blanket over his little body when he slipped over to the other side. That visual has been with me my entire life.

The reality is that our time here on earth will not last for-ever, so every minute is precious. Once we gain perspective about our own mortality, realizing that our time is limited, we have the opportunity to accomplish important things for our family and our community. And since we usually do not know how much time we have, we must work hard today to accomplish those things.

For children, time seems to stand still, and they act as though their lives will never end. For adults, time seems to fly by, and there is never enough time to get everything done. The children we hold in our arms grow up much too quickly. Each new day brings greater purpose for living. But with each day, death is ever closer; we just try to ignore it.

To many, death comes without a warning. In the case of my childhood friend Andrew, he and his family knew he probably would not survive his cancer. But, like Andrew, we must fight on and make the most of the time we have.

Why is this concept meaningful to me? I was not ex-pected to survive my first year. I was born with a severe heart defect that required emergency surgery when I was less than one day old. At age thirteen, when I developed a bacterial infection of my heart that nearly took my life, cardiologists were unsure of my future. Fortunately, a gifted surgeon found a solution and saved my life. The following year when

I had reconstructive open-heart surgery—a procedure known as a Fontan procedure—and received a pacemaker, there were complications, and my own mortality was ever present. I knew that one day I would need a heart transplant in order to survive. When I asked my parents why I was still alive, they would say, "You must have been put on this earth for a reason." In my opinion, what my parents told me applies to every person living today. Each of us has been put on this earth for a specific purpose, and part of our task in life is to discover that purpose.

Most people try to avoid talking about death or even thinking about it. Many fear death because of the unknown—perhaps because they do not understand or believe in a Supreme Being or a divine plan. But developing a relationship with God has helped me and millions of other people understand the purpose of mortal life. I believe that acknowledging the reality of death can be a great motivator. None of us really knows when our life will end. After all, there is no expiration date on our birth certificate. We could die tomorrow or many years from now, and, of course, we could shorten our time here by acting recklessly.

In summer 2008, doctors told me that without a heart transplant, I would not survive. Thoughts of my wife living without me and of my daughter, Eden, growing up without a father tore me apart. If it weren't for my family, I would be fine with dying. After years of facing death, I don't fear it because I have come to understand that it is part of a larger plan and purpose for all of us. But because of my love for my wife and daughter and my responsibilities as a husband and father, I was determined to do all I could to survive.

What transpired over the next year gave me the opportunity to look back at life and reflect on the many wonderful things my family and I have been blessed to enjoy. I learned a great deal about my family, my community, my God, and myself.

As I took this journey—as I waited for my heart transplant—I wrote down my thoughts, feelings, and observations. I started an online blog called Living for Eden, named after my daughter. The main purpose of the blog was to update my family and friends. Within a month I decided to make the blog public. My career as an award-winning pianist and recording artist meant I received a lot of interest from concerned people throughout the world who were sending me e-mails. In the beginning everything seemed to focus around my suffering and me. However, as days turned into months while I waited for doctors to find me a heart, a whole new world opened up to me, and I found great happiness in the time I had been given. I began corresponding with hundreds of families in similar situations who were looking for hope amid despair.

My hope is that these weekly blog entries will inspire you. If you are looking for answers to some of life's most important questions, perhaps this book will help. While the thoughts expressed in these blog entries are mine, I believe the principles are universal to those who appreciate spiritual things.

Chapter 1

LIVING FOR EDEN

PART 1

My Future

On Tuesday, I will find out what the plan is for my future. Will I need a heart transplant, or will I need some other major surgery? Either way, I am going downhill and something needs to be done to keep me alive. I'm exhausted. I'm wearing oxygen all day, but it hasn't helped me feel better. Climbing the stairs to my bedroom is a challenge. I lie around most of the day. At night, it's hard to sleep lying down. I'm using three or four pillows so I can breathe comfortably.

I had a cardiac catheterization a few days ago. From this test, cardiologists will be able to determine my future. I was put completely under for the procedure, which was performed in what looked like an operating room. My muscles were temporarily paralyzed so I would not move. A doctor inserted a needle in the femoral artery in my left leg and then

In heart failure, I was prescribed oxygen 24/7.

threaded a small tube through the artery. Next, dye was injected in the artery so doctors could map out my heart and view things they couldn't see externally. They learned that the left side of my heart is functioning very well and, miraculously, is beating in sinus rhythm (normal heart rhythm). I usually have an irregular heartbeat. The other side of my heart, my deformed right atrium, is expanding like a balloon. It is full of blood that swirls around and around but never really goes anywhere—at least not in a timely fashion. There is no room left for the atrium to expand further. In fact, my right lung is collapsing from the pressure. The ballooning atrium is cutting off blood flow to my lungs, so less oxygen makes it to my cells.

After the procedure, the anesthetist gave me a little something to help my body start up again, and as I awoke I felt quite uncomfortable. The tube that had helped me breathe during the test was removed from my throat, and at that point we ran into a serious problem. For nearly two hours, I battled for my life, trying to breathe. My lungs would not work properly, and I felt like I was drowning or had a bag over my head, suffocating. I flung my arms around, trying to grab on to something while my anesthesiologist tried to help me breathe using a bag. Eventually, I could breathe normally again. I'm glad it's over and that my medical team now has the information they need to evaluate my case.

I've been blessed my whole life to have this heart defect. I am far from perfect and believe that I needed this in my life to teach me things that I could never have learned without it. I want to live a long time and enjoy my family and the life I've been blessed with. With every struggle, I continue to be reminded of my Savior, who has undergone far greater suffering so that the human race would not have to suffer forever in pain and grief. Jesus took this burden upon Himself, and our mortal suffering is temporary. While in my own moment of suffering, all I could do to hang on and stay optimistic was to think of Jesus hanging on the cross, trying to catch His own breath, until it was time for Him to die. There is nothing I could go through to ever compare to what He has done for the world. I love Him for it, and this knowledge helps me face an unknown future. I know everything works out according to His plan of happiness and His purpose for each of us.

AUGUST 6, 2008

Possible Heart Transplant

After reviewing my tests from last week's procedure, my adult congenital cardiologist, Angela Yetman, told my wife, Lynnette, and me what needs to happen. Thursday, I meet with the heart-lung transplant team to begin further testing and discussion to determine if I qualify for a heart transplant. This news is very sobering for us, but we have hope and faith in God's great plan of happiness.

Most of the doctors in our community who are familiar with my case believe I should have the transplant as soon as possible because of the severe damage to my right atrium. Although a couple of cardiologists I've spoken with have been even more blunt in relation to me having a transplant. They've said, "You won't survive a transplant." They've suggested another option—where my damaged heart would be reconstructed—but that has been ruled out because my body is not strong enough. Regardless, by the end of the year I may be having major open-heart surgery. If I get a transplant, there is a good chance I will live a little longer and be able to enjoy all that is beautiful in this world. If I undergo the alternate operation, a majority of my cardiologists, especially my adult congenital cardiologist, believe I won't have a chance.

As we left the hospital with such heavy news, feeling incredibly humbled at where we are in our lives, everything outside seemed more beautiful. Even the music on the radio felt more alive. Thoughts of dying bring everything wonderful into focus. All is well, and I'm reminded of the last verse to a hymn called "There Is a Green Hill Far Away:"

> *Oh, dearly, dearly has he loved!*
> *And we must love him too,*
> *And trust in his redeeming blood,*
> *And try his works to do.[1]*

AUGUST 18, 2008
Meeting the Transplant Team

My wife and I, along with my parents, met with Latoya, a coordinator with the heart-lung transplant team. We went over all of the aspects of being listed and receiving a heart. A lot of work goes into the process. One is required to be in somewhat good condition so the heart will not be rejected. There are about thirty people on the list in Utah. There is over a 90 percent survival rate for the first year for those patients whose anatomy was previously normal. I'm not sure what the statistics are for people like me. On Tuesday, the transplant team will present my case before the board, and there will be a vote. I'll know in a few days if I'm approved. But I'm confident it will go through. The various tests and all the blood work my transplant cardiologist, Dale Renlund, has ordered don't bother me because I know if I get a new heart I'll have more time with my wife and two-year-old daughter.

I have received nothing but support from family and friends. People are so good to us. And I thank everyone for their faith and prayers on my behalf. I have begun to pray each day for the family whose tragedy and sacrifice will create new life and another chance for my family and me. It's an interesting thing to pray for. It's ironic. This is similar to a couple waiting to adopt a child. They're praying to take the baby from its own mother, which seems awful. Yet, these ironies in life somehow bring about the purposes of God. Whoever my donor will be, I know he or she is an angel, and I'll think about that person every day for the rest of my life and beyond.

AUGUST 20, 2008

Great News!

We got a call this morning from Latoya, informing us that I am now listed for a new heart. Wow! This is really amazing to be at this point of my life—sobering and surreal. On Friday, I get a pager, and the transplant team will be able to contact me at any time. It might be two weeks before I get a heart, or it might be a year. Dr. Renlund thinks it's going to be a while, probably a year, because there are a lot of people waiting. The heart needs to come from within a 500-square-mile radius of Salt Lake City. When the team has a match for my body, the pager will go off, and I will head to the hospital with my 72-hour kit (the things I want to have with me

Shortly before being listed for a heart transplant (Paul, Eden Joy, Lynnette).

during recovery). I will have one hour to get to the hospital. In the meantime, a thoracic surgeon will travel to where the new heart is and carefully remove it from the donor. He or she will have a good idea from there if it will be a perfect match, and if it is, they'll prep me for surgery. The thoracic surgeon will bring the new heart to the hospital where my surgeon will remove my bad heart.

This is a very difficult surgery because of my heart's anatomy. Once the surgeon goes into my chest, he will find a lot of scar tissue from the surgeries I had earlier in my life. Finding the good tissue among the bad will be tough. He will have to cut in the right places. We have every confidence in the transplant team and in the surgeons.

What gives me comfort and peace? The love I feel from my wife, my family, and my friends. Through our family and community, we feel the arms of God around us. I also find great comfort in my faith. I know that God lives. He is my friend.

How can I face a possible death? Because I believe that we lived with God before we were born, that He sent us here to experience life in a physical body, and that when we die we go home having learned more about ourselves and our Father in Heaven.

During life's journey some of us may need a physical heart transplant but we must also, all of us, experience a spiritual heart transplant. I strive for that every day of my life because I know I am far from perfect in many of the traits I want to improve on, such as kindness and friendship. But through consecutive acts of goodness we may begin the process of having a spiritual heart transplant because of God's love and guidance in our lives.

I don't fear dying. I remember meeting with one of my former surgeons, Donald Doty, years ago to discuss my unknown future. He is a man I greatly admire not only as a physician but as a spiritual leader in our community. I told him I was not afraid to die. He looked at Lynnette and then looked me deep in the eyes. While pointing to Lynnette, he said the words I'll never forget, "What about her? If you die, what about her?" I was put in my place, as I should have been. It's one thing not to fear death; it's another to excuse the feelings of those left behind to grieve. Of course, I didn't want to leave Lynnette behind, but now I understood a deeper purpose in living. Lynnette is everything to me, and I want to be around to love and support her.

Chapter 2

MY WIFE, LYNNETTE

It was music that brought my wife, Lynnette, and me together. The day I spent in her home learning piano techniques from her brother Ryan, she and a friend entered the room just long enough for me to take notice.

Although I am nearly four years older than Lynnette, when we were teenagers I was attracted to her spunky personality, elegant smile, love of music, beautiful green eyes, blonde hair, and endless energy. But there was something deeper that pulled me in. She had lost her mother when she was eight years old, and that tragedy had made a woman out of a girl. Lynnette was independent and took responsibility for her education, her work, and her spirituality. At an early age, she had developed a deep love for God.

While on my Church mission, I occasionally asked my brother Brian about Lynnette through letters, as they were good friends. When I returned two years later, she was at my home with friends. She came in and sat next to me at the

Lynnette as a toddler.

piano while I was playing some tune I don't even remember. I stopped playing and we talked. An hour seemed like a minute. I felt like we connected on every level, and I wanted to talk more.

Several weeks later, I was late for a church meeting, and Lynnette was sitting on the back row of the chapel. No one was sitting by this attractive girl so, as a single guy, I felt obligated to do so. As I sat down, Lynnette said to me with some sarcasm, "And I thought I was late." I don't think either of us remembers what was said in church on that Sunday. I'm sure it was something meaningful and probably inspired people. What I do remember is that I realized right then how my relationship with Lynnette had changed over the years and that it was quite different now that we were adults. I asked her

Lynnette and I at our wedding reception April 11, 1997.

out on a date, and she said yes. From that day on we were inseparable friends, and we were anxious to learn everything about each other.

My wife is inspiring, beautiful, strong in spirit, graceful, elegant, kind, thoughtful, helpful, full of love, caring, tender, talented, gifted, and so much more. When I asked her to marry me, she exclaimed, "It's about time!"

"No kidding!" I replied. While sitting on the couch, I told her how much I loved her and that I wanted to be with her not just for this lifetime but beyond into eternity.

I thank God every day for leading me to her. I'm not sure we each have a soul mate, but I'm certain that loyalty to true love creates soul mates.

❧ *Chapter 3* ❧

LIVING FOR EDEN
PART 2

THURSDAY, SEPTEMBER 4, 2008
Three Weeks on the List

Three weeks ago I was listed for a heart transplant. Because of the complex nature of my anatomy, my blood type, and the other people waiting, doctors say it could be up to a year before I get a call informing us a donor heart has become available. Yet, as we are faced with this enormous challenge, my wife and I feel a sense of comfort and peace that we have prayed for through this process.

We will struggle financially, since I won't be in a position to carry on with my work due to the exhaustion and fatigue I experience. I own a small record label that I run from my home, and I also consult with musicians and record piano CDs each year.

For the past sixteen months, we have been in a financial position to extend our insurance through COBRA, to allow

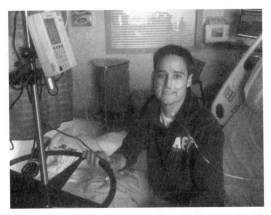

Trying to stay optimistic while receiving 24/7 medical care at a local hospital.

my wife to cut back on hours and stay home to do what she loves most, which is being a wife and a mother. We feel our dedication to one another is why God has blessed us with the ability to pay our bills and get by. We don't need things. We have each other.

Our hope was that I'd find insurance through my work, but then I became sick. As a result, Lynnette is going back to work so we can continue to receive medical insurance as well as supplemental income.

Eden and I are sad to see Lynnette leave a couple of times a week to go to work. We love having her home. Lynnette is a registered nurse and works in a newborn intensive care unit, or NICU. If my own child were in the hospital, I couldn't ask for a better, kinder, more caring nurse. Lynnette is very good at what she does. I admire her abilities.

When my wife and I were engaged to be married, several people wondered if she was making the right decision tying the knot with a man with a severe heart defect who might not be around very long. Her own mother passed away from a five-year battle with cancer when Lynnette was only eight years old, leaving her father—a wonderful, humble school-teacher—to raise their ten children alone. Life hasn't always been easy for my wife. However, with a sense of passion in her heart she would tell people who asked such a question, "But I love him. He's worth the risk."

We have a dedicated and loving family who is going to help me care for Eden while Lynnette is at work. My daughter, with all of her beautiful energy of life, can be a bit overwhelming for a father with my level of fatigue.

As I experience the symptoms of heart failure and wait patiently for the call that could change our lives forever, I need to express my appreciation to God for the challenges I've had throughout my life. Looking back on past experiences where I was near death, I believe it is because of my family's faith in a loving, kind, and understanding Heavenly Father that my family was strengthened and grew closer together during difficult times.

You can't know the sweetness in life without tasting the bitterness also. There is no reason to blame God for what we are subjected to. I believe we chose to experience earthly life as part of a three-act play in the eternal nature of things. I believe we lived with God in the first act. We are in the second act. God knows what's ahead for us in the third and final

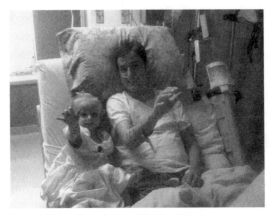

Eden's hospital visits cheered me up. She loved lying next to me in my bed.

act after we die. Like any loving parent, He enjoys seeing us grow and mature from the good choices we make.

At times we make poor choices or are hurt by the choices of others. But I'm convinced there is a loving Savior who wipes away our tears and heals our wounds.

WEDNESDAY, SEPTEMBER 10, 2008

Crank that Pacemaker!

Today Dr. Yetman had pacemaker technicians crank my pacemaker up to give me a better rhythm to help with my fatigue. In addition, Dr. Yetman prescribed prednisone, a form of steroid, to help my body absorb protein. For some reason, I have developed a side effect from the Fontan procedure I had when I was fourteen—something called protein-losing enteropathy (PLE). It's a condition where the body does not absorb protein as it should. I'm still learning what that means, but I know it involves my enlarged liver and spleen, which are congested because my heart is failing. In August, my transplant cardiologist, Dale Renlund, told me I wouldn't survive very long with end-stage heart failure and protein-losing enteropathy.

Nevertheless, life is good. Eden is very imaginative these days. She is in the princess stage of dress-ups and crowns. She wears these colorful outfits and refuses to take them off.

Late last night after a church service project, Eden noticed how tired I was and, acting like her kind mother, she said to me, "You wear your oxygen," followed by, "Lie down, Daddy." She asked me if I wanted to watch a show. Obviously, my sweet two-year-old is concerned about my illness. But she wouldn't know anything different; this is all she's known.

THURSDAY, SEPTEMBER 11, 2008
North Shore

Sometimes I wonder why I can't be back on the North Shore of Oahu, Hawaii, waiting for a heart. Lynnette and I love spending time on that beautiful island, where there is such an overwhelming feeling of peace. Can't they let me sit on the beach, drinking ice-cold lemonade, and have me paged

Enjoying the cool sand on the North Shore of Oahu
shortly before being listed for a heart transplant.

if a heart becomes available? Possibly charter a really fast jet to land on Kamehameha Highway? Maybe I wouldn't make it back in time. So much for my brilliant idea of lying under the tropical sun on a beach waiting for a heart!

SATURDAY, SEPTEMBER 20, 2008

Your Heart vs. My Heart

So what is normal? On pages 276–77, you'll see the progression of my heart and then what a normal heart looks like. As you can tell, I have no right ventricle. Oh well. To my understanding, the non-oxygenated blood comes from my body into what looks like a balloon, but is actually a homemade right atrium. The non-oxygenated blood then swirls around like a European roundabout and flows, hopefully, out to the lungs. Normally, there are two valves for the non-oxygenated blood to flow through. But I was born with a poorly functioning tricuspid valve. I was told I had tricuspid atresia and later learned my condition is known as double inlet left ventricle. In addition, my main arteries, or the greater arteries, were reversed at birth, so I was also diagnosed with transposition of the greater arteries, or TGA. But when I was born, the doctors carefully figured out how to replumb blood flow so I could survive.

Five weeks ago, I was listed for a transplant. I felt okay as long as I lay around most of the time; if I did much of anything else, I became tired very quickly. In an effort to resolve this fatigue, cardiologists turned up my pacemaker to a minimum of seventy-five beats per minute and increased medications. In the beginning, I felt wonderful, but today my legs and stomach are increasingly swollen. I have edema in my belly, thighs, legs, and ankles.

Despite the minor setback, I have to thank everyone for all their prayers and fasting on my behalf. I can literally feel the arms of God around me through your prayers, service, and love. There is great power in prayers, and they are answered. My positive attitude or feeling like everything will work out is because of prayers. I'm overwhelmed by the support we have received.

Three-Day Hospital Stay

When doctors started me on steroids two weeks ago, my blood sugar shot up from 100 to 450. This is very dangerous. My stomach and legs expanded with fluids from all parts of my body. Basically, I retained water. Doctors ordered me to the hospital for end-stage heart failure treatment.

I felt like Violet, one of the characters from the book *Willy Wonka and the Chocolate Factory.* She rebelliously chewed on a piece of gum after being told not to. Then she blew up like a blueberry and had to be taken to the squeezing room for de-juicing. That is how I felt. "Please somebody poke me with a pin to let all this air out," I said.

Thankfully, my experience was not as horrible as Violet's. In fact, after three days of treatments I went home with IV diuretics to get rid of all the excess water. I have spent a lot of time in the bathroom. In addition, I was given protein infusions to replace my protein stores and a blood transfusion to replace red blood cells.

Doctors are slowly taking me off the steroids because they're not working to resolve the serious issue of my body being unable to absorb protein. The biggest concern for my medical team has been the protein-losing enteropathy (PLE). Statistics and doctors suggest that the PLE will lead to my death unless a transplant takes place. A new heart in my body might cure me of this dreaded disease, and then my enlarged liver would reduce to a normal size.

Holding Eden after returning from a trip through Europe.
The swelling in my face is a symptom of severe heart failure.

WEDNESDAY, OCTOBER 1, 2008
Medication Time

In order to keep myself alive, I am taking a lot of medications.

THURSDAY, OCTOBER 23, 2008
Back in the Hospital

After being home for a couple of weeks, my health has declined once again and I have had to be admitted to the hospital. My water retention is worse. I'm more tired than I've ever been. I'd been dragging around and all I could do

Primary Children's Medical Center in Salt Lake City, Utah.

was lie down. I was too tired to watch television. Because of the difficulty in caring for me at an adult hospital, my care has now been transferred to Primary Children's Medical Center, since the pediatric cardiologists who specialize in the complex nature of my congenital anatomy practice there.

The other wonderful medical center has little experience in caring for adults with congenital heart disease. They are well-versed in heart failure and heart attacks, but my unique anatomy requires the attention of pediatric cardiothoracic surgeons and congenital heart specialists. This will not be a typical heart transplant. It's very complicated. As part of this innovative plan, I will continue to receive all of my care at Primary Children's Medical Center until all post-transplant and all congenital problems have been resolved.

I am anxious to get back home. I miss home. But I realize this is all part of a grander plan to get me healthy.

On Monday, I'm scheduled for a couple of minor procedures, including a cardiac catheterization where doctors will put in a stent to help get more blood flow to my lungs. My pulmonary artery is being crushed by my huge right atrium. In addition, they are considering upgrading my pacemaker.

This is all temporary, and it is all part of an effort to keep me strong so I can survive the transplant when that happens.

Thanks for all your thoughts and prayers. I know they are heard because I am not yet depressed or feeling anxiety. I am hoping the Lord's plan for me is to stay here longer.

SATURDAY, OCTOBER 25, 2008
Home for the Weekend

After a difficult week of being in the hospital to help me with my exhaustion, my cardiologist pulled some strings to get me home for the weekend. Eden has been sleeping at my parents' home and at my sister-in-law's home. My wife has been working. I am happy to be with them for this short weekend.

Tomorrow, after church and a nap, my wife will work a night shift. I'll be with my daughter at my parents' house overnight before I go back to the hospital on Monday for several more days of procedures and some minor surgery, where doctors will perform another cardiac catheterization and put

Lying next to Lynnette with my oxygen tank I called R2D2,
at my parents' home one Sunday evening.

a stent into one of my arteries. They may also change my
pacemaker. Then I expect to recover for a few days.

While I was in the hospital, they inserted a PICC line (a
peripherally inserted central catheter, a form of intravenous
access that can be used for a prolonged time) so that I can be
on full-time IV medication. I'm taking Lovenox shots twice
a day to thin my blood so I don't throw a clot and have a
stroke. In addition, the Lovenox might help my protein-losing enteropathy. I am wearing a defibrillator life vest twenty-
four hours a day in the event I have a serious arrhythmia or
a heart attack. The jacket is extremely uncomfortable. It is
like sleeping on four rocks and a thin hardcover book. I'd
like to ditch the vest. Because of the new need for an IV

medication, I was moved up on the waiting list, which will help me get a heart sooner rather than later.

The hard reality that is finally sinking into my brain is that I am very sick. I think I've run my entire life on adrenalin or optimism. When I think about my situation, I can get frustrated. It's sometimes difficult having limited mobility. I'm not allowed to drive with the life vest, and I rely heavily on my wife and family for support. But I know God has blessed me. Though there is pain and suffering, I know that He cares for all those who are hurting. I am one of the many millions of people hurting, and I trust He knows what He is doing.

We feel His love and strength through the service of others. It's so important to strengthen our family relationships. There will come a time when you will need them. I am grateful for mine. I wish everyone had the support I do. But sadly, many do not, and it breaks my heart. We need to reach out to those in need.

On a spiritual note, there were a couple of things this week in the hospital that helped me a great deal. The first is the principle of prayer. There were nights in the hospital where I felt like I wouldn't be able to make it through the night. Having a prayer with my wife, and on another night my mother, and on another my father, brought solace. Depression faded. I felt peace and comfort from that simple principle of opening up my heart to God, counting all of my blessings, and thanking Him for all that is good in my life.

The second principle that helped me this week is hope.

Dieter F. Uchtdorf, one of the presiding leaders of the church I'm a member of, gave a beautiful message about hope. He said, "Hope has the power to fill our lives with happiness (see Psalm 146:5). Its absence—when this desire of our heart is delayed—can make 'the heart sick' (Proverbs 13:12)."[1] President Uchtdorf is from Germany and grew up during World War II. His father was off fighting the war and his mother was left to move the family around to keep them safe. She implanted hope in her children's hearts. President Uchtdorf's words of comfort have implanted hope in my heart.

NOVEMBER 4, 2008

Getting Out

For the first time in months, I was finally able to get out of my home and do something other than travel to a hospital. This felt great, like I had some control over my life. I chose to go vote in our political election. Afterwards, a friend and I went to the drive-through at the local Crown Burger. I probably shouldn't have indulged in a large, juicy burger but I jokingly said to my friend, "They're taking my heart out anyway." In addition, Lynnette and Eden and I went to my sister's home so my daughter could go trick-or-treating with her cousins. Who would have thought that my little girl, the one who is always dressing up like a princess, would go as a spider for Halloween? She cracks me up. Eden and her smile make all thoughts of illness disappear.

I saw Dr. Yetman today, and she said things looked stable. I'm giving myself Lovenox shots twice a day in my abdomen to help me absorb protein. I'm wearing oxygen 24/7 at three liters, and I carry around in a fanny pack a bag of Milrinone, which is pumped through my PICC line into my vein. With all of these devices, it is hard for me to shower. However, despite all of these minor burdens, I'm grateful these things are available to help me stay alive long enough to get a second chance at life after we find a heart.

Through all of this, I was moved up on the transplant waiting list from a 2 to a 1-B. What does that mean? You're either a 7, 2, 1-B, or 1-A (I guess because they can't count from 1 to 4). To my understanding, and I might be wrong, 7s are people who have qualified for a heart but, because of other circumstances such as additional disease, infection, extreme obesity, or other medical factors, they are on temporary list status. People who are 2s need a heart soon but not immediately. They are managing somewhat comfortably or at least are stable at home and they are able to go to work. People become 1-B when they keep going in and out of the hospital for various reasons. They receive medication through a PICC line twenty-four hours a day and have other issues. When you are in need of a new heart immediately and doctors believe that you will not survive long without a heart, you are listed above everyone else no matter how long you or anyone else has been listed, except for those who became 1-A before you did.

NOVEMBER 9, 2008
Cabin Fever!

I have cabin fever, like a person stuck on an island. I'm able to move around the house, but it's becoming exhausting to leave the house. I spend my day listening to music, sleeping, listening to my daughter play (which is my favorite part of the day), watching *The Price is Right* and 24-hour news, reading the Bible, the Book of Mormon, and other interesting books, and watching the clock.

NOVEMBER 18, 2008
Ninety Days on the List

My health has been steady the past two weeks since the heart cath I received. And I realized I've been on the waiting list since August 20. That's somewhere around ninety days! I'm sure I've got ninety or more to go until I get a call. There's no doubt this holiday season will be very special for our family.

Sitting at home, I've had a lot of time to reflect, and I watched a video I've shown at my piano concerts that comprises some old film footage of me as a child with my sisters and little brother. Old family films are nostalgic. My family has always been the rock of my life. They continue to sacrifice their time and energy to help Lynnette and me with our daughter and countless other things. I wish everyone could have this comfort in their lives. It's unfortunate that some people have no family.

NOVEMBER 26, 2008
Happy Thanksgiving!

At this time of year I'm extremely thankful to all of you for your thoughts, prayers, and fasting. I'm at peace with my health and look forward to living the next chapter of my life. But I'm so happy to be feeling better than I was several weeks ago when all I was doing was lying on the couch, in bed, or in the hospital.

This time of year is very meaningful to all of us, and I'm happy to have most of my family in town to help enjoy my favorite meal: cooked turkey wings and legs, mashed potatoes, gravy, stuffing, veggies, and pumpkin pie.

God is so good to us even if we are going through difficult times. Incidentally, I was able to go to church this past weekend. Because I hadn't attended for several months, I had almost forgotten how special the feeling is there. The warmth of people who love God and who have love and friendship for each other is something I wish everyone could enjoy. I know God loves us, and we can feel that peace from

Him during our trials if we work within ourselves to let Him in. From my experience, it's expressing and focusing on pure gratitude and thanksgiving for all the things in our lives— regardless of our difficult circumstances—that bring His love into our hearts.

DECEMBER 3, 2008

106 Days on the List—All is Well

One hundred and six days on the list. Fifteen weeks. All is well. Any predictions?

Despite the minor physical anxieties of waiting for a heart, always wearing oxygen, taking a bazillion pills, giving myself shots twice a day, and carrying around a bag of medication going directly into a permanent IV in my right arm, I have the larger anxieties experienced by those who are sick for a long time and happily married. Keep in mind that I'm too tired to stay busy, so all I have to do all day is think and reflect. Above all, I hope my wife—the love of my life—is happy and fulfilled, and that she feels appreciated for her sacrifice, service, and love.

My dad, a journalist, once interviewed one of my heroes, Howard W. Hunter, who was president of The Church of Jesus Christ of Latter-day Saints and a community giant. President Hunter was soft-spoken and humble despite his enormous list of credentials and accomplishments. In the interview, my dad asked about all the years President Hunter tenderly cared for his sick wife, who later died in a rest home. "How were you able to do that all those years?" my dad asked.

President Hunter paused. Then with moist eyes and emotion in his voice, he said, "She would have done the same thing for me."

I'm reminded of an experience I had one day at Bryner Clinic in Salt Lake City. While I waited to see my family doctor, I observed a feeble old woman waiting for the pharmacist to complete her prescription. She was with her husband. They were both petite, weak, and very old. She sat in a wheelchair and was so tired that her head kept falling backward. I watched her husband, who stood by her side, hold up her head, even though his hands shook and they had to wait for some time. I think he held her head for twenty minutes. Watching this tender act of kindness—although the man himself was weak—left me with a lasting impression on how I want to love and serve my wife.

While serving a mission in California for the LDS Church, I was responsible for several missionaries, two of whom were an old couple serving in a small mining town. Like all of our missionaries, they were responsible for knocking on doors and sharing a message of love about Jesus Christ. The wife had really bad arthritis and bad knees. Often she couldn't use her legs because of the pain, but she didn't want to give up. Her husband drove them in the car from house to house. He would get out and knock on the door while his wife waited. If people invited him in, he'd go to the car, open the door, pick up his wife, and carry her into the home so they could do what they loved to do most, which was to bring hope to people through their message.

These experiences—my observations of love in action between couples—are always on my mind. And I hope I get the chance to show the same expression of love and service to my wife who has so kindly sacrificed, served, and loved me through this current life challenge. It is much easier to serve than to be served.

❧ *Chapter 4* ❧

GROWING UP THE SON
OF A NEWSMAN

*H*oward W. Hunter was one of the many people my
father has been fortunate to interview. You see, I grew up
the son of newsman in the glory days of television when
there were only a few channels to choose from. Even before
I was born, my father, Duane Cardall, worked as a journalist for KSL Channel 5, the local CBS affiliate in Utah. With
my dad's talents and strong, articulate voice, he could have
moved us around the country for more glamorous positions
and higher salaries. But he has always been a family man,
devoted to his wife, children, church, and community.

In the 1970s, while television reporters still captured
events on reel-to-reel film, my father gravitated toward cover-
ing religion, later becoming the religion specialist. Over the
next three decades, Dad would bring the latest news and
information from The Church of Jesus Christ of Latter-day
Saints (Mormon) headquarters in Salt Lake City, into the living rooms of viewers throughout the Rocky Mountain region.

In 1979 my parents traveled to Israel with LDS Church President Spencer W.
Kimball as part of my dad's news assignment. Standing outside the Garden Tomb
are Spencer W. Kimball, Camilla Kimball, and Duane and Margaret Cardall.

Though he is a devout member of our church, Dad always
remained objective in his reporting. He was what you might
call an old-school Walter Cronkite.

As part of his assignments with KSL, Dad interviewed
and traveled the world with LDS Church presidents. When
my father began his career at KSL in 1972, the LDS Church
had 3 million members. When he ended his religion-report-
ing assignment after nearly thirty years, the Church had almost 12 million members. Today there are almost 14 million.
According to *US News & World Report,* "Mormonism is the
fastest growing faith group in American history and if present
trends continue there could be 265 million members of The
Church of Jesus Christ of Latter-day Saints (LDS) worldwide by 2080."[1]

Doug Robinson of the *Deseret News* wrote the following article about my father in 2006.

> [Duane] Cardall has been embraced by President Spencer W. Kimball. He has stood side by side with President Gordon B. Hinckley in a soldiers' graveyard and watched tears roll down his cheeks. He observed Ezra Taft Benson tell Donny Osmond to get a haircut. He has seen things he says he can't tell because he considers them sacred.
>
> From 1969 to 1998 Cardall covered the church, which meant he became acquainted with seven of the church's 15 presidents—David O. McKay, Joseph Fielding Smith, Harold B. Lee, Spencer W. Kimball, Ezra Taft Benson, Howard W. Hunter and Gordon B. Hinckley. They taught him many things; for one thing, he learned never to underestimate the energy of older men.
>
> They ran him ragged as he followed them around the world to some 55 nations. "It was exhausting," he says. A full night's sleep was rare, what with the demands of travel and the limits of the technology at the time. He had to rely on airline pilots to take his film to Salt Lake City from wherever he happened to be in the world at the time.
>
> There isn't room here to do his experiences justice, but Cardall, now editorial director of KSL, riffs through the memories during a brief conversation. He once accompanied President Hinckley on a visit to his ancestral home in England and while they gazed out at the sea together the church leader told him, "You ought to go

up the road to Gravesend and do a story on Pocahontas. She was buried there."

Says Cardall, "The Disney movie about Pocahontas was just about to be released. He knew there would be interest in that at the time. He's very much aware of contemporary culture and society. I wound up doing a story on Pocahontas."

His most poignant moment with President Hinckley came when he accompanied him on a visit to an American cemetery in Manila. As they stood there he recalled that he had dedicated the land of the Philippines 40 years earlier when there was one member of the church there. Now there were a half-million.

"Just a few of us went out there," says Cardall. "He stood on that spot and recounted the experience. It was extremely emotional. He had tears in his eyes."

Cardall has particularly fond memories of President Kimball, a diminutive man with a history of illness that led many to believe his presidency would be short-lived. He served 12 years, all of it at a virtual sprint that took him to 40 nations.

"First of all there was his utter humility and will-ingness to reach out to people," says Cardall. "He embraced people and kissed them on the cheek and said, 'I love you.' I experienced it first-hand. . . . He was the prophet of the people. He traveled on buses instead of limousines. He interacted with people and people loved him."

There were light moments along the way. He was standing near President Benson at a highbrow reception in England to celebrate the 150th anniversary of the church in that nation. The president was in a receiving line greeting well-wishers when Osmond came along. "Young man, you need a haircut," he told him.

Looking back, Cardall wraps it up eloquently when he says, "For nearly three decades I had the privilege of having a front-row seat as these church leaders traversed the world, guiding the remarkable growth of the LDS Church. Personally, it was a gratifying experience and, professionally, it was simply a great story."[2]

I remember my dad telling me about his first trip accompanying President Spencer W. Kimball. Despite the prophet's advanced age and a long list of medical problems, he desired to be out among the members of the growing Church. While en route to Sweden for a conference of the Church, President Kimball's party had a layover at the airport in New York City. In the VIP waiting room, most of the traveling party gathered around the president, while my father, feeling a bit insecure and self-conscious, took a seat across the room.

As my father watched the large circle of people surrounding the prophet, President Kimball noticed him there sitting alone. Soon Arthur Haycock, the president's secretary, left the circle and walked toward my father. He said, "Duane, President Kimball wants you to come join him. He doesn't want to leave anyone out of his circle."

This was a simple act of kindness and an expression of love and concern from a great leader to a humble television reporter, who, in my opinion, is the greatest father around.

鈴 *Chapter 5* 鈴

LIVING FOR EDEN

PART 3

Ridin' the Hoveround in Costco

I can't believe how much fun it is to drive a Hoveround scooter all over Costco. I had noticed how much fun the folks seem to have in the Hoveround commercials—often shown during *The Price is Right,* which I watch almost every day—but I never realized it was true. The other thing that amazes me is that you can scoot around Costco in less than twenty minutes and still spend almost $500.

On a serious note, in regards to my PLE (protein-losing enteropathy), I finally learned the importance of avoiding food that is high in fat. The more fatty foods I eat, the more protein I lose from my system. I am also losing a lot of blood in my intestinal tract. This is another contributor to my anemia. I'm quite pale. (I realize the vampire craze is popular

With a PICC line in my right arm and an oxygen tube running into
my nose, I managed to help decorate our Christmas tree.

but this is a little ridiculous.) I'm seriously motivated to eat less fat and continue eating a ton of protein.

At Costco, I bought some 30-gram protein bars and shakes. I am also eating a lot of meat, eggs, and anything else with protein. Of course, it is still difficult to avoid all fat.

Overall, it's been a good week. I'm stable, and I was fortunate to ride a scooter in Costco with everyone staring at me like I had stolen it from an old woman. You can still enjoy life, even though you're dying!

DECEMBER 19, 2008
The Blessings of Christmas

Two months ago, all I could do was lie around because doctors were trying to figure out how to get my heart failure under control. I was in need of a serious tune-up. Whether it's a consequence or not, I was humbled to learn that my family, friends, fans of my music, and those I don't even know began praying for me.

I want everyone to know that God is good to me and loves you, because for the past two weeks, as we get closer to Christmas, I have felt great. Not 100 percent, but well enough to get out a few hours each day. Well enough to make gingerbread houses with my kid. Well enough to laugh and enjoy this time of year. And it's because of prayer and the wisdom of my doctors that I am tuned up for a time. And what better time than Christmas!

Prayer is a gift. The opportunity to talk to God every day and know He is listening is a gift. Life is a gift. Family is a gift. And I am more than happy this particular time of year to celebrate the birth of our Lord.

Chapter 6

MEMORY OF A CHRISTMAS PAST

$\mathcal{M}$any years ago my parents gave my brothers and sisters a wonderful gift by shaking up our family tradition of opening presents around the tree. On Christmas Day in 1990, my dad and mom made a special announcement to our family. Since my twin sisters—my oldest siblings—had recently married, there were twelve in our family. Dad said, "Next holiday season we're going to forgo having Christmas in our home."

My mother added, "We're going to go somewhere." Of course, we were excited, thinking Mom and Dad were finally going to take us to Hawaii. But they explained that we would take the money they would have spent on gifts and travel to a city in Mexico and give much needed clothing, supplies, and toys to a couple of orphanages. It's very difficult to make all of us speechless, but at this news, we were.

As the season grew closer, our family gathered each Sunday in our weekly family counsel to discuss the trip. Dad brought out the map and showed us a route from our home to a city called Chihuahua, which is located several hours south of El Paso, Texas, in the heart of Mexico.

"We're driving?" said someone.

"That's right," said Dad. "We're taking Grandpa Layton's big red truck and we'll use our van." Dad and Mom planned to put all the supplies in the truck along with a few of us while the rest drove in the van. They said, "We'll stay with Uncle Jim Cardall's family in Albuquerque, and Aunt Cathy Richards's family in El Paso, until we get down to Mexico." I can't say we kids were too thrilled.

Our long road trips were not a scene out of *The Brady Bunch*. We didn't sing "Kumbaya" together. We mostly teased each other, argued, tried to sleep, complained of being hungry (or ate the tuna or peanut butter and jelly sandwiches Mom made), passed around the cookies with a "take one" policy, climbed over the seats and each other, and whined about the smells. Every now and then there was some peace and meaningful discussion. Dad likes historical monuments and markers, so we'd have to stop to see all of those things. One thing I enjoyed was the one cassette tape in the car—a mix of old John Denver tunes.

Anyway, a week before Christmas in 1991, we loaded up the truck. Dad had contacted the humanitarian department of our church, which provided several large, heavy, crate-like packets of clothing and blankets all tightly bundled in white canvas and secured with haywire. We had also gathered supplies from our neighbors, friends, and family. People were very generous. Overall, we had enough clothing to stock a Salvation Army store.

The only person in our family who spoke Spanish at the time was my new brother-in-law, Dustin Child. He had learned the language while serving a Church mission to Ecuador and Florida. (Since then my three brothers learned Spanish serving missions to Spain, Chile, and Florida. I didn't serve a Spanish-speaking mission, but I did study Spanish in high school.) For the memorable journey, Dustin would serve as our interpreter and drive the truck with all of its supplies. Meanwhile, Dad drove the van.

After saying good-bye in El Paso to our relatives, we approached the Mexican border at Juárez. Government security quickly moved vehicles through. By now, most of us had become quite excited and anxious. I was seeing a part of the world I had never before seen. We were on an adventure and experiencing something special.

Finally, we made it to Chihuahua, the capital of the Mexican state of Chihuahua. The city, then home to half a million people, thrived with commercial industry, and we saw people walking, driving, and biking everywhere. Unfortunately, the city had a high rate of property crime, especially theft and graffiti.

Our family checked into a motel and grabbed some food in a restaurant. Afterward, we joined some kids playing soccer in a nearby field. This was one of my first experiences with people from another culture, and although we didn't speak the same language, we all laughed, kicked the ball around, and had a good time.

In the morning, my parents drove us to the first orphanage, but the gated facility looked abandoned. The surrounding walls were tagged with graffiti, and broken glass covered the top of the walls. We were disappointed and concerned. Dad suggested we make our way to the contact whose name had been given to us by a helpful humanitarian organization.

We found him in a small building adjacent to the hospital, involved in a service project helping people who couldn't afford medical care. When I learned his name was Jesús, I felt we were in good hands. As we entered the building, we saw several people lying in beds. A beautiful new baby had just been born to a pretty girl. We took turns holding the baby and did our best to communicate with the patients.

Because the orphanage had been closed, we decided to provide the medical facility with blankets. We brought them in from the truck and placed one on each of the beds. This small act of service brought us children a sense of satisfaction and happiness that really can't be described in words.

Later we drove to the second orphanage, where a large number of children played in the schoolyard. They greeted us with big smiles, and we spent the next few hours playing with them.

I will never forget walking through the orphanage and seeing bedrooms where children bunked together on small beds, side by side, like a scene out of *Annie*. As I soaked in the atmosphere of concrete walls, hard floors, a dirt

The Cardall family in Chihuahua, Mexico with Jesús, a service volunteer
and his family (Margaret and Brian Cardall, Jesús and family, David,
Jane, Duane, Paul, Caron Cardall Child, Craig in front).

playground, and the children's innocent faces, I felt sad-
dened and confused. Why would people abandon their children? How could a parent leave a child? I was angry.

Now that I've grown older and seen many similar situations, I'm comforted by a verse in the Bible where the Savior
describes His love for His children despite their circumstances. Isaiah 49:15 reads, "Can a woman forget her suck-
ing child, that she should not have compassion on the son of
her womb?" There is nothing more tender than the love that
exists between a new mother and her baby. I believe the Lord
uses this powerful analogy because a mother's love is sacred
and special—there is nothing like it. Yet there are circumstances where women and men do lose their love for their

children, and that is when neglect begins. The Lord continues, "Yea, they may forget, yet will I not forget thee." These comforting words reveal the depth of the Lord's love for us. He will not forget us. He will never neglect us. He knows us, and He understands. My favorite verse of scripture follows in verse 16, where the Savior of the world says, "Behold, I have graven thee upon the palms of my hands; thy walls are continually before me." Our hearts, our very lives, everything we deal with in this life, every emotion and challenge, all of our problems are continually in the Lord's thoughts. He knows each neglected child and will help each one who seeks Him out. My parents taught us to seek out the neglected, serve them, and show them God's love.

On that trip, my family spent Christmas Eve in an orphanage with almost fifty beautiful Mexican children, each one with a smile on his or her face. We took all of the supplies we had gathered and put them in one room like a store. The children lined up and freely "shopped" for shoes, pants, dresses, shirts, and more. Afterward, we enjoyed a wonderful dinner as the children brought us our food. Later the children performed several native Mexican Christmas songs. As we all sang "Silent Night," a special feeling came into the room—a feeling I can't describe. Thinking back now, it reminds me of how I felt the day I was married and the day my daughter, Eden, was born. In fact, I've felt God's love on many occasions since that Christmas Eve in Mexico. It was a spirit of unity, of love, and of mutual respect. I enjoyed

Christmas that year with my "brothers and sisters," many of whom I had never met before that trip.

What surprised me about this whole experience was that as we tried to serve others, we were the ones being served. With their big brown eyes, large smiles, talents, and expressions of love, these children served us. They brought us food, entertained us, and allowed us into their lives for an evening. I learned more about the possibilities of this world in that experience than in all the years before. My parents were brilliant to orchestrate an event that would strengthen our own resolve to give to others and to appreciate all that we've been blessed with materially. We never felt richer than when we were in Chihuahua, among the Mexican people.

✣ Chapter 7 ✣

LIVING FOR EDEN

PART 4

DECEMBER 26, 2008 PART ONE

A Heart for Christmas—or Not

The call came at 12:45 A.M. "We have a heart for you," the voice on the other line said. I was in shock. I had prepared for the call but, because it came early Christmas morning and because it was *real*, it left me speechless and emotional. We had until 2:00 A.M. to get to the hospital. The operation would take place at either 6:00 or 7:00 A.M. I called my parents to meet us at the hospital. They called my siblings to let them know what was going on. Earlier that night, we had all gathered with the husbands, wives, and kids for our annual Christmas Eve dinner at my parents. It was a great night. We had a special family prayer and the kids acted out the nativity scene. Lynnette, Eden, and I left to go home at 11:00 P.M. Before putting Eden to bed, we each opened a present. After

Eden was tucked away in her bed, Santa came. Then the phone rang.

We arrived at the hospital feeling a great sense of peace and comfort. The time had come, and I was ready. Nurses began the preparations. Everyone was extremely positive and saying things such as "Merry Christmas!" and "What a great Christmas gift!"

A rather large IV was inserted in the arm opposite my PICC line, and a lot of blood was drawn from my already-existing PICC line for lab work. They had me wash my chest and groin area (where the major arteries are for the heart-lung machine) with special medical soap. It was a little cold. Then two pediatric thoracic surgeons, Drs. John Hawkins and Peter Kouretas, came into my room a little before 5:00 A.M. and told my wife and my parents what was expected. Dr. Hawkins mentioned the difficulty of my particular case because of my heart's anatomy. It would be challenging to get the old heart out. There would be a lot of bleeding. He said, "There is an 80 percent chance we'll have to go back in later to stop the bleeding." He said that chances were I might not make it. The harsh realities left me a little depressed, but I still felt peace. While I already understood the dangers of the procedure, when I was minutes away from it actually happening, life became quite sobering.

They came to get me at 5:20 A.M., and before the anesthesiologist took me into the operating room I talked briefly with my wife and parents. I kissed Lynnette, told her how much I love her, and then headed down the hallway to the operating room.

LATER COMMENTARY

Up to this monumental moment, for some reason God had preserved my life and allowed me to enjoy this beautiful world. Would this be it? Would I go on? At this point my medical team, family, and I were completely uncertain, and we all realized I was in the hands of the Creator. I felt as if I'd been pushed out of an airplane with no parachute. All of my past medical history and what led to this moment went through my mind. As I was wheeled off to a life-changing surgery, time stood still.

Chapter 8

A BROKEN HEART

*T*he problems of the world cannot possibly be solved by skeptics or cynics whose horizons are limited by obvious realities. We need men and women who can dream of things that never were," said John F. Kennedy.[1]

The popular scientific philosophy of the late nineteenth century did not keep Norwegian surgeon Axel Cappelen from trying to save a young twenty-year-old man who had received a stab wound to the left side of his chest. "A surgeon who tries to suture a heart wound deserves to lose the esteem of his colleagues," said world-renowned Austrian surgeon Theodore Billroth in 1881.[2] "Surgery of the heart has probably reached the limits set by nature," wrote English surgeon Stephen Paget in his popular 1896 book *Surgery of the Chest*.[3] There were no x-rays, anesthesiologists, or fancy equipment. These major obstacles did not keep Dr. Cappelen from making his way into the young man's chest through the ribs, where he successfully sutured a wounded heart. The entire medical community was inspired, and this act gave them hope in the ability to save more lives. The men and women who go forward in faith with perseverance like Dr. Cappelen—despite the odds stacked against them—are the ones who bring about miracles and change in our world. Without such innovative and determined people, I would not have survived thirty-six years on only a single ventricle, or as we called it as I was growing up, half a heart.

For obvious reasons, I have no personal recollection of what happened the day I was born, but from everything I've been told, I shouldn't have lived more than a few days.

In the evening of April 24, 1973, my mother's labor and my arrival on this mortal stage were routine. I arrived a few weeks past her due date, and I weighed nine pounds thirteen ounces. But within hours, the nurses attending to me knew something was wrong. I was born a "blue baby." The bluish color of my lips and body suggested that the blood flowing through my circulatory system did not contain enough oxygen to sustain my life. The most likely cause was a serious problem with my heart.

The medical team at LDS Hospital in Salt Lake City, Utah, knew I needed the attention of pediatric specialists. Not many hours after my birth, as dawn was about to break, I was transported by ambulance to nearby Primary Children's Hospital (now known as Primary Children's Medical Center). There I came under the skilled care of a pioneering pediatric cardiologist by the name of Dr. George Veasy. An external examination suggested a very serious, even life-threatening,

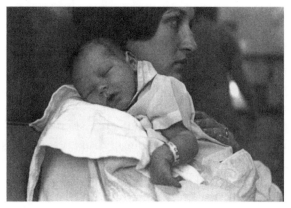

My mother, Margaret Layton Cardall, holding me days
after my first open heart surgery in April 1973.

heart defect. A more thorough diagnosis would require a procedure to see inside my body and my tiny heart. But before I
would undergo my first heart catheterization, my father and
grandfather arrived at the hospital. Although time was of the
essence, Dr. Veasy allowed these two men to take me into a
small custodian's closet where they could have some privacy.
In that closet, they placed their hands on my head and gave
me a priesthood blessing, according to the practices of our
LDS faith.

The heart catheterization confirmed the physicians'
worst fears. My heart was a mess. The official diagnosis was
"double inlet left ventricle." In short, I had a single ventricle.
In a normal heart, two ventricles pump blood—one to the
lungs where the blood is oxygenated, and the other to the

body to sustain life. In addition, my major vessels were transposed, one of my two atria was malformed, and some valves weren't functioning properly. Without immediate surgical intervention, I was doomed.

The proposed surgery was incredibly risky, but doctors determined there was no other choice. My father tells the story of sitting outside Dr. Veasy's office shortly after the diagnosis was made and overhearing a telephone conversation between the doctor and our family's physician, Dr. Luther Giddings. "Lou," my father heard Dr. Veasy say, "this kid isn't going to make it."

Twenty-two hours after my birth, I was taken into the operating room, where a gifted pediatric thoracic surgeon, Dr. Conrad Jensen, created a connection between the artery to the left lung and the aorta, the large artery that supplies blood to the lower half of the body. In medical literature, this procedure is known as a Potts Shunt, in honor of Dr. Willis J. Potts, a Chicago surgeon who devised the operation in 1946.[4] The small man-made opening between the two great arteries increased the blood flow through my lungs, improving the general oxygenation of the blood. Dr. Jensen saved my young life.

While lying in the newborn intensive care unit, my parents were unsure of my future. Howard W. Hunter, a prominent leader of our faith, was in the hospital one day giving a blessing to another child on the floor, and my dad recognized him. He felt inspired to ask Elder Hunter to also bless me. My parents recall that a peaceful feeling entered the room

*The Duane and Margaret Cardall Family in 1974
(Paul, Margaret, Caron, Carol, Duane, Rebecca).*

with this man. He counseled my parents and told them my heart defect was not their fault. He then blessed me and said I would live to be a man. All those involved in my care were deeply comforted.

Ten days later, my parents took me home to my three older sisters, all under the age of four. They were in awe of what doctors had done for me, and they were grateful to God for the miracle He had orchestrated. Despite the miracle, Dr. Veasy implied I would need a major operation at some point to keep me alive, possibly ten to fifteen years later if I survived the first year.

Although congenital heart disease was the world's leading birth defect, my parents didn't know anyone else who had a child like me. They simply assumed their boy was special.

My first grade school picture.

There was no support group, no Internet, and in those days chronic illness was something you just didn't talk about.

My parents were told to keep me home and out of public contact for twelve months, yet my mother still had her fears. In the middle of the night, when she would check on me lying in my crib, she was terrified that she would discover I wasn't breathing.

When my pregnant mother and I arrived at our semi-annual appointment the following year, my doctor, who became known to me later as Uncle George, looked at my mom's belly and said with some concern, "What are you thinking?"

Of course, my young mother confidently said, "We're going to have another child." George Veasy, with his silver white hair, thick-rimmed glasses, and white coat, didn't say much after that. My mother and I returned with my new brother David a few years later. After observing the interaction between the two of us, Uncle George said to Mom, "I need to apologize to you. This younger sibling is the greatest thing that's happened to your little boy."

My parents didn't have time to treat me differently, particularly after adding two brothers and another sister to our family, a total of eight children. I have always appreciated that they treated me like any other kid. I wasn't kept inside or prevented from playing with other children. Whether I played neighborhood games like kick the can or bike tag, or dug to China in the sand pile, I was active and happy. When people asked about my scar, we'd tell them that, as a matter of fact, I had only half a heart. It didn't matter. I was happy and enjoying my childhood.

Mom made my annual doctors' appointments a fun experience. On the way home, she always took me down the hills of the Avenues a little faster, so that when we went over the bumps, it felt like we were flying. She'd stop at the Hostess store off 7th East in Salt Lake City to get my favorite treat, pink snowballs.

In my eighth year, I had a battle with pneumonia that sent me to a children's hospital for several days. I should have looked forward to missing school as a child but not when I was feeling so achy and dull. Being away from family and friends in a room shared with another patient—a complete stranger—scared me. The nurses were kind to me, but I was not familiar with my surroundings, and I remember feeling alone the first night. The following day I was joined by a new patient, a diabetic teenager who was interesting and fun to talk to.

The Boy Scouts of America program was a big deal in our neighborhood and in our extended family. My grandfather, Alan Layton, a construction man by trade and a former artillery captain during World War II, served as president of the Great Salt Lake Boy Scout Council. He encouraged Scouting in our family because it stressed principles of trust, loyalty, charity, kindness, respect, obedience, integrity, survival, and hard work. However, Scouting required strenuous activities like hiking and other outdoor activities.

Earning the coveted mile swim was a challenge, but I was determined to make it happen. Several scouts registered at Olympus High School in Salt Lake City, where we began taking thirty-minute classes to prepare for the swim. A neighbor, an older gentleman, was our instructor. We discussed my heart problem and he said, "If you get tired swimming in the deep, go to the side of the pool and grab onto the ledge to rest. It's okay."

Each class, we would spend our time swimming a few laps and trying to swim in the same spot of the deep end for an extended period of time. We were being taught endurance and survival. One lesson required us to jump into the deep end of the pool with all our clothes on. We had to make

The evening I received the coveted Boy Scouts of America Eagle Award, age thirteen.

flotation devices out of our pants by tying them in knots in sections and blowing into the pants. This task was very hard because I was already struggling just to breathe and to stay afloat. I'll admit, training to survive in deep water seemed hopeless and impossible in my condition, but I was still determined to swim a mile no matter how hard it was. I made many trips to the side of the pool to catch my breath and rest. My friends were supportive and never laughed or made fun of my health. They encouraged me.

Finally, the day came to swim the seventy or so laps that made up a mile. Although the other boys were told to swim without stopping, I was on the edge of the pool so I could grab onto the side if I needed to. It was extremely hard for me, but I kept going. I frequently grabbed the edge so that I could catch my breath, but dragging myself along a pool edge for a mile was still quite a workout. The others finished way ahead of me, but eventually I completed the mile. I was grateful I did not give up, and I am thankful for leaders and parents who supported my goals.

Living with a heart defect never deterred me from my desire to become an Eagle Scout. My half heart could not stop me from trying as hard as I could to keep up with the other boys, even if I was the last Scout up the mountain. I convinced myself that my middle-aged scoutmaster, who was also my uncle and backyard neighbor, appreciated having someone along who was a little slower than the others. We stopped to rest plenty of times, and I was grateful to eventually meet up with the other scouts. I loved to sit around the campfire with my friends, sharing stupid jokes, scary stories, and learning wisdom from our leaders.

Eventually, at age thirteen, I completed all of the requirements, earned enough merit badges, and was honored as an Eagle Scout among my family and friends. I join with all those who've earned this award in thanking the many leaders and parents who devote their time and energy to strengthening youth.

Life couldn't have been better. What we didn't know the night of the Eagle Award celebration was that one week later

I would fall deathly ill and end up back in the hospital, facing an unknown future.

As the illness hit, all I could do was lie around the house, complain about my chest hurting, and suffer with flu-like symptoms. My mother and father wondered, is it the flu or pneumonia? I lost fifteen to twenty pounds in a matter of a few weeks. I was depressed. I missed my friends and attending school. During these challenging weeks, my grandfather Layton brought me a special gift. He knew I was down on myself and not improving, and I was even too ill to open the gift. My mom unwrapped the package and handed me a football signed by all of the football players of Olympus High who had won the state championship in 1984, two years earlier. Grandpa had been given the football after making a donation to the school's athletic program. His giving it to me meant a great deal.

I was not getting any better. Our family doctor, Lou Giddings, checked me into Cottonwood Hospital, which was close to our home south of Salt Lake City. But after a couple of days of x-rays, blood work, and a variety of medications, they were unsure how to treat me. Stumped and discouraged with my lack of progress, Uncle George (Dr. Veasy) said, "Get that kid up here." The ambulance ride to Primary Children's Hospital on the north end of Salt Lake City should have been fun for a thirteen-year-old boy, but I was too miserable to think about it or even remember that it took place.

At Primary Children's Hospital, a blood test revealed that I had staphylococcal bacteria circulating in my blood. The medical term is *staphylococcal septicemia,* commonly called blood poisoning. The doctors began treating me with antibiotics. The infectious-disease doctors at the hospital worked with Dr. Veasy to combat the staphylococcus bacteria that were consuming my heart, but the doctors couldn't determine the source of the infection. As the days progressed, the antibiotic treatments did not help. I was getting more and more ill, and I was losing more weight.

Dr. Veasy, a man who devoted his entire life to the care of young children, had become discouraged with my situation. Knowing our family's devotion to God and to our church, this kind and wonderful doctor wanted to do something beyond what he was doing in the hospital. He went home and walked across his lawn to knock on his neighbor's door. He asked his neighbor if he'd be willing to come and visit a sick patient in the hospital. The gentleman consented. I remember lying in my bed very weak and in pain, with my parents there comforting me, when Dr. Veasy and Elder Howard W. Hunter walked in. I don't remember what was said, but I remember Elder Hunter, who I believe was one of God's handpicked spiritual leaders, gently laying his hands on my head and offering a tender blessing. He said, "You are in the hands of the Lord." Once more, the man comforted us and reaffirmed our faith in our Heavenly Father's eternal plan. Elder Hunter would later become the president of The Church of Jesus Christ of Latter-day Saints.

Finally, doctors decided to try a new radiology test called the MRI (magnetic resonance imaging). This innovative device uses a strong magnetic field to create the diagnostic images. The scanner had arrived in Utah six months previously and was housed in a trailer at an adjacent adult hospital down the hill from Primary Children's. On three different occasions, I was taken by ambulance to the trailer and scanned with the MRI. When the images from the third MRI were analyzed, doctors realized that I had a walnut-size blister of staphylococcal infection in my Potts Shunt—the shunt that had been created on the day of my birth. Once again, doctors determined that without urgent surgery, I would die.

When we asked our thoracic surgeon, Donald Doty, how he planned to repair my heart, he replied, "I don't know. I'll go home and think about it and come back tomorrow with an answer."

Needless to say, this was a stressful time for our family. While we expected the best, we also began planning for the worst.

As a teenager stuck in a hospital, I missed school and hanging out with friends. To add to my own stress, I overheard Uncle George say to other doctors while on rounds, "If we don't act quickly, I'm not sure that kid is going to make it."

Our family had hope that the Lord would bless me, and, as in previous times, we trusted in His divine will. We exercised all the faith we could muster. Friends and extended family helped out with my four sisters and three brothers while my parents stayed at my bedside. During this time, I developed a strong relationship with my parents. We spent a lot of time praying.

The evening before my critical surgery, while I was at the hospital, my family gathered at home, on their knees, and prayed as a family to our Heavenly Father. According to my father, my younger brother Brian who would have been about nine years old, pleaded with the Lord in prayer as he "bawled like a baby" for his older brother's life.

In the morning, Dr. Doty walked into my hospital room with a confident look on his face. He said enthusiastically to my parents, "I have thought about this complex problem and have received confirmation that the plan I have devised will work." He then went on to explain that in order to gain control of the infection, the staphylococcal abscess must be cleaned out and repaired, and the Potts shunt closed to prevent recurrence of infection. The diameter of the Potts shunt had expanded over time so that high blood flow had caused high blood pressure in the arteries to the lungs.

He continued, "Paul can't live without some form of shunt but it cannot be made of artificial materials because of the risk of infection. It must be made from his own tissues, and it needs to be one which will allow the blood pressure in the lungs to decrease. We are going to construct a new shunt conduit fashioned from a vein which we will remove from his leg. The natural vein won't be large enough, so we will cut the vein open through its length, then wrap it around a tube in spiral fashion and stitch it back together to make a new conduit that will be exactly the right diameter and length to provide some resistance to flow while allowing sufficient flow to enter the lungs at reduced blood pressure. We have had considerable experience with this type of spiral vein graft for bypass of large veins but have not used it previously as a shunt conduit for congenital heart defects. I am confident that it will work."

We knew that this talented surgeon had looked beyond his own abilities and asked God what to do, and that a revolutionary procedure had been revealed to him. Once again I was a pioneer patient.

I hugged my parents nervously and was wheeled off to the operating room. I remember being anxious to get the sickness out of my body so I could go back to school. I also turned my thoughts to God and the faith I had that I would live. I was willing to deal with whatever came my way.

I spent many hours in the operating room, but the Lord had sustained my life, and the surgery was successful. We were thrilled and grateful to God for His kindness. The experience seemed to be a gift because of how it brought our family together in a unique way. We built a solid foundation of faith, and we had a memory to fall back upon when other things in our lives went sour. To create such a bond between family members was well worth what I went through, and I would do it again in an instant. I went home in time for Christmas. However, Dr. Doty informed us that I would need additional surgery to reconstruct my damaged heart. He had removed the infection, but we needed to wait for my heart to heal before he could go back in. Dr. Doty explained that

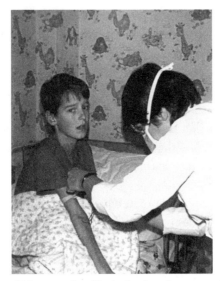

A phlebotomist taking blood a few days after my second
open heart surgery in November 1986, age thirteen.

I might be a little more blue and that my exertion could be
somewhat compromised compared to before the operation
because the blood flow to the lungs had been reduced by the
smaller size of the new shunt.

Going back to school was difficult. I was so tired, and I
knew I'd be getting reconstructive surgery when school was
out for the summer. I was worried about climbing the stairs
in my school to reach my last class. I had tried to arrange
all of my morning classes to be on the first floor so I could
make it on time. Stairs were hard to climb because I would

get nauseated from exhaustion. My heart had been repaired, but it was working really hard to keep me going. One day, I slowly made my way up the stairs to my health course, of all classes. I sat near the back. A few minutes into the class, our instructor stared at me and said, "Are you okay? You're very pale."

I asked if I could see her outside. In that empty hallway, looking at my health instructor, I broke down for the first time in months. Up until then I had been strong and unable to show emotion. I don't know if I had been strengthened or numbed during my ordeal, but I finally broke. I started crying and I stuttered, "I had open heart surgery a month ago. I'm nauseated and tired."

This wonderful woman first apologized for drawing attention to me, and then she led me downstairs to the teacher's lounge, where I could lay on the couch. She got me a drink out of the vending machine and some food. "It's okay if you're late," she said. "Take your time going up the stairs and I'll have a drink of water for you when you get up here." I was grateful for her kindness in helping me feel normal.

School turned into a wonderful memory. Kids were kind. Some of the cute girls gave me a nickname since I looked a little blue and purple in my lips and fingernails, which is not uncommon in congenital heart patients. They called me Purple Plum. When a cute girl calls you anything you're happy. I was encouraged to run for a student body office, and several people helped me with my campaign. I won and looked forward to the following year.

By August, a repeat cardiac catheterization confirmed that blood pressure in my lungs was reduced enough to allow the reconstruction operation to be performed. The new shunt had been just right. This was a miracle, because had I not gotten the infection and needed a new shunt that was smaller, I would likely have just lived with the old Potts shunt until my lungs were completely destroyed. Then nothing could have been done for me.

In late August, my thoracic surgeons reconstructed my heart using a procedure called a modified Fontan procedure. Fontan was a French surgeon who conceived the idea that the venous blood returning to the heart from the body could be shunted directly into the arteries leading to the lung and bypass the heart completely, leaving a single ventricle heart to pump solely to the body. Blood flow through the lungs was due to venous pressure being somewhat higher than normal. This venous pressure abnormality eventually took its toll later in my life, but that August Dr. Doty reentered my chest, took down the lifesaving shunt fashioned from my leg vein, and connected the right side filling chamber (atrium) directly to the pulmonary artery.

The operation went well, and for the first time in my life, I had pink color on my lips and fingernails. My family believed I would be in and out of the hospital in seven to ten days, but there were minor complications and my chest had to be reopened two more times to resolve issues with a faulty pacemaker. Reliving surgery again and having my sternum reopened three times was not a fun experience. After my chest had been reopened twice, I was not thrilled when doctors said they had to go back in a third time to fix leads connected to the pacemaker. I'd had enough. I was tired. I was depressed. I was angry. As I was wheeled back into the operating room, I asked my father to let me go. I told him, "I just want to die."

With great sternness, my dad said, "You go in there and get taken care of. You are not going to die."

After all the complications were resolved and I began feeling well, I was thankful for my dad encouraging me. I also felt really strong. The newly reconstructed heart allowed more oxygenated blood flow in my body. I still wasn't able to go to high altitudes for a long time, where exercise was involved, but I was happy to be alive and thrilled with an opportunity to enjoy life as a teenager.

As a teenager reflecting on the challenges our family had faced, I learned that we relied on God more than ever for strength and help. In the dark moments, when I was too tired to pray or even to think positively, I'd found myself asking why the Lord had forgotten me. But eventually I began to understand the depth of His love, and how each of us can feel Him in our lives if we pay close attention and listen for His gentle, soft voice. I believed He carried my burden through those weeks of illness and on the operating table. Despite these assurances, I was still a typical teenager who had a lot to learn about God.

A few weeks after my four surgeries, I got on my knees in my bedroom and opened up my heart in prayer to my

Heavenly Father. I thanked Him for allowing me to feel His love and kindness, and for getting me through the difficult surgeries. Then, as humbly as I could, I said to Him, "Please Lord, if it be according to your will, I want to live long enough to tell people here on earth you are real and that you love them." I continued, "Let me serve a mission when I am older. I want to spread Thy gospel door-to-door." Before I closed the prayer I said, "You can take me when you need me. Whether I'm over here or over there I just want to tell the world about your never-ending kindness."

🦕 *Chapter 9* 🦕

LIVING FOR EDEN

PART 5

DECEMBER 26, 2008, PART TWO

A Heart for Christmas—or Not

In the cold, brightly lit operating room, nurses lifted me from my bed onto that firm, narrow operating table I had become familiar with over the years. I received a dose of Versed for anxiety and preparation. Before they would put me completely under, we were waiting to hear from one of the surgeons, who had gone to check out the donor heart to make sure everything was absolutely perfect and good to go. About thirty minutes later, the news came. The new heart had a problem that had been undetected until my surgeons looked at the organ themselves. The heart had an aneurysm, which would require additional surgery on top of everything else we were dealing with.

The surgery was called off. I didn't know what to feel. Shock? Relief? Disappointment? I felt all of those things.

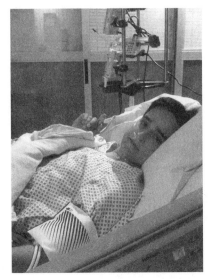

*Waiting to go to the operating room to have a heart
transplant early Christmas morning 2008.*

Lynnette and I came home five hours later on Christmas morning. My daughter, who had been taken care of by my sister-in-law, asked if I brought her a sucker from the hospital, and things seemed back to normal. I was anxious to experience Santa with my child. One of the gifts from Santa to Eden was a Fisher Price medical kit. She practiced giving shots to me and listening to my heartbeat.

I am thankful for the love and support of my family and friends, particularly my sweet wife.

I am going through a roller coaster of emotions. In a way,

this experience seems like a brief second opportunity before we find out the real outcome of my life's journey. Every musician needs a dress rehearsal. I am ready for another call, but for now I'll enjoy this weekend with my wife and daughter as we humbly celebrate the birth of the Babe in Bethlehem some 2,000 years ago. Inspired by our sobering moment, these words of poetry came to me and I wrote them down.

> *Time, precious time,*
> *How quickly the leaves fall from the tree.*
> *Time, oh precious time,*
> *In a blink of an eye a child grows old.*
> *And in the pursuit of joy and happiness*
> *Lies time*
> *But quickly it fades*
> *And all we have are memories,*
> *Precious moments,*
> *Remembered in time.*

FRIDAY, DECEMBER 26, 2008
An Eventful and Unforgettable Christmas

BY LYNNETTE CARDALL

Though I have no problem publicly sharing some aspects of my life, I contemplated sharing our recent Christmas experience. Paul shared it on his blog and he always puts it so well that I did not feel I needed to share it on mine. The feelings and fears that accompany the experience of Paul awaiting a heart transplant are feelings I would rather keep to myself. But this blog is for journaling purposes, and I have been so inspired by many other bloggers who are experiencing their own kinds of adversity and trials that I feel it would be okay to share my side of the story.

Early Christmas morning, around 1:00 A.M., the phone rang. We joked that some idiot was going to feel really bad when the machine came on, and they realized they had the wrong number. But then Paul's cell phone rang, and I knew it was the call we had been waiting for. We all thought what a miraculous Christmas gift it was, and we joked that it was going to make a great book or Hallmark movie someday. We scrambled to get a few things packed, and I called my sister to come stay with Eden.

Santa had already made a stop at our house, and the thought that Christmas morning with Eden was not going to happen occurred to us. You put a lot of work into being able to witness a few prized moments on Christmas morning, and I didn't want Paul to miss it (or to miss it myself), so we woke Eden up to open a few gifts. We were so rushed we didn't even take pictures. Paul had me open one gift before we left. It was a heart pendant necklace (so appropriate). I cried.

We kissed Eden good-bye and headed to the hospital. We were so incredibly nervous that we both nearly threw up in the car as we drove. Good thing I didn't throw up, though, because the van was my other Christmas present, which I had received only a few days before. Paul had traded in his beloved BMW (uh, lemon!) and surprised me with a Toyota Sienna. It's not a car I would have bought myself, but now I love, love, love it! Way to go, babe! (Yes, I am joining the ranks of you minivan moms.)

Anyway, we met Paul's parents, his brother, and his brother's wife in the lobby. Oh, it was good to see them. Paul's dad and brother gave us both blessings. And over the next three hours, the hospital prepped Paul for the surgery, did blood work, and even gave him a dose of immunosuppressant drugs. The surgeons had all stopped in his room to talk to us, and at one point the main surgeon sat down to discuss the seriousness of the surgery. We have always known it was a risky surgery, but at this point hearing more about it only added to our nervousness. My being a nurse didn't help either. I've had a few bad (and, I should add, teary) nights at home after combing through medical journals about statistics of transplant patients like Paul. At one point, I had to convince myself to stop looking and turn completely to hope and faith, because that is really what I needed to get through this. This surgeon was just doing his job, and I appreciate his frankness, but it was rather bad timing.

By about 5:30 A.M., Paul was heading to the O.R. At this point I was really sick—I can't remember a time feeling this anxious. I kept wondering if I had said everything I wanted to say to Paul just in case I didn't have a chance to say it again. I just couldn't think straight! We sent him off, and I was so glad Paul's parents were there to go crazy waiting with me. We began to relax, but only a little, now that we had surrendered to the whole ordeal.

About twenty minutes later, the surgeons came to the waiting room to inform us that the surgeon retrieving the donor heart had found an aneurysm on it that they had not picked up on the echocardiogram. They were perplexed, as they had not encountered this before. They were not sure what they were going to do. At least they had not cut Paul open yet. When they left to go study the situation, we were discouraged and confused. We sat there wondering what to do, feeling tired, anxious, and sick all at the same time. I just prayed and prayed. The doctor returned after what felt like forever and said they had decided to not use the heart. I worried how Paul would react when he became aware of this, but as he came out of the light sedation he was at peace. Besides, now we could enjoy part of Christmas Day at home.

We all have prayed for the right heart to come at the right time under the best circumstances. This obviously was not the right heart for Paul. I know that God watches over all of us. I pray that Paul will have many years left to enjoy life, but if the Lord has another plan I will accept that too. I think Paul will be fine and I hope for that, but we still have to address these thoughts when faced with such serious circumstances. Some days I don't think I'm strong enough for this, and someday I may have to retire to a loony bin, but I know I wouldn't have chosen not to marry Paul because of this. I wouldn't want to give up any of our time together for an easier lot. Paul is who I needed, now and in the eternities.

My nurse and wife, Lynnette, changed my PICC line dressing each week.

JANUARY 3, 2009

Pick Your PICC Lines

This was a week of PICC lines. (Incidentally, I should be grateful. Having a PICC line with a good source of Milrinone does make me feel better. So, being connected to a tube full time is not that bad.) I went in to the hospital on Monday because the area where I received my original PICC in my right arm six weeks ago was becoming irritated and red. We don't want an infection, so we decided to pull the PICC and put a new one in my left arm. Only this time I was not sedated, so I do remember the experience. Most adults aren't sedated, but I'm sort of a baby when it comes to needles and wires being threaded through my veins so I usually beg for it. This time, I manned up and went for it without sedation. We did the procedure in the cath lab. Needless to say, they gave me several shots that numb the skin before inserting the wiring and the eventual PICC. It was similar to the dentist numbing your gums before he drills. It wasn't that bad, and I went home thirty minutes later. Of course, my wife heard me say the whole ride home, "That wasn't fun." Oh well, I was happy to be home.

After a few hours we noticed the leak—a watery substance coming from where the PICC was inserted. Lynnette, who is my home-health care nurse (lucky me), ended up changing the dressing six times over the next few days because of the leaking. Then yesterday I went in and had that PICC removed and a new one placed in my right arm above my elbow, where the original one was. Needless to say, the big needle wasn't that bad and I made it home to watch the University of Utah destroy Alabama in a much-deserved bowl game. Let's just hope this new PICC doesn't leak either. It's only been a little more than twelve hours.

JANUARY 8, 2009
Primary Children's Medical Center

I am fortunate to receive all of my care from the good folks at Primary Children's Medical Center in Salt Lake City, Utah. I'm thirty-five but the oldest baby on the planet, so they oblige. Actually, all of the experts and surgeons who specialize in my heart's anatomy and birth defect are there. I grew up going to this hospital when it was high up in the Avenues of Salt Lake, above the state capitol building and the Salt Lake Temple. Now, it is located on the University of Utah campus and next to University Hospital, where a lot of advances in medicine are being developed.

Every time I go to Primary Children's Medical Center, I am deeply affected by the number of ill children I see. They are so helpless and hurting. Many are scared, and some are alone. I remember being there myself as a child and having the same emotions. But there could not be a better place or staff to accommodate them and their families. These children bring a special feeling to the place. I believe angels walk the halls and provide a comforting spirit.

I'm also amazed at the advances in medicine since I was a child. When I went last week to have my PICC replaced in radiology, I saw a hallway with a sign that read MRI. This was incredible because when I was thirteen with a potentially fatal staph infection in my heart, we had to travel to LDS Hospital in an ambulance so I could have an MRI. In fact, the MRI had only been there in Utah for six months. The full body scan was able to help doctors locate my staph infection and prepare the surgeons, which prolonged my life. Amazingly, when I was there two months ago in intensive care, a nurse whom I had not seen since I was fourteen came to my bedside and we had a great discussion. There are many great folks who are still there, and they remember the kids.

I'm very honored and feel greatly blessed to receive my

Playing the piano with a fellow patient at Primary Children's Medical Center.

care from the staff at Primary Children's Medical Center. As one of their patients, I feel like a black sheep among some of God's purest sons and daughters. When you pray this week, keep in mind the kids up there in that hospital, even though we don't know their names, faces, or stories.

No More Handshaking

Doctors suggest I wash my hands often and try to avoid shaking hands with people. They also tell me to avoid large groups of people because I am extremely immuno-suppressed, and anything could get me sick. If this happens, it will postpone the heart transplant. I need to stay free of all bugs. This is tough because I enjoy being with my large family and attending church, where the people there are my other family.

Chapter 10

THIS DISEASE COULD KILL ME

IRON DEFICIENCY

Because of my heart failure I am anemic. So for the past five days I have received an iron transfusion through an IV each morning for an hour, in addition to the gazillion other medications I am taking.

Iron deficiency is the most common deficiency disease worldwide. More than 1 billion people have iron deficiency, and about 700 million people have iron-deficiency anemia. Iron is an essential nutrient for every human cell. It plays a valuable role in the transport and storage of oxygen and oxidative metabolism, and in cell growth and proliferation.

Venofer® is used to replenish body iron stores in patients with iron deficiency. It is also a brown, sterile, aqueous complex of polynuclear iron (III)-hydroxide. But I told my daughter it was chocolate medicine.

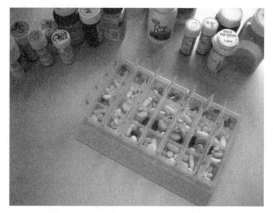

The various medications prolonging my life.

PROTEIN-LOSING ENTEROPATHY

I also have PLE, which is the main reason we're in a rush to get a heart. This disease could eventually kill me.

Dr. Anji Yetman helped me understand this a bit better. Here is her explanation: "PLE is characterized by severe loss of proteins from the gut. Normally, very little protein is lost through the gut but with PLE, protein loss from the intestines may reach extreme levels. Basically, the inner walls of the intestines become leaky, allowing protein to leak into the gut and exit the body. The body requires adequate protein levels to hold fluid within vessels. In the face of low protein levels, fluid leaves the vessels, leading to swelling. In addition, protein is needed to make substances in the body which fight against infection. With significantly low-protein levels, the body's immune system is compromised and serious life-threatening infection may occur.

"PLE can occur as a complication of several different diseases, but in patients with congenital heart disease it typically occurs following the Fontan surgery. Why some patients experience this complication and others do not remains a bit of a medical mystery.

"Following the Fontan procedure, there are abnormal flow patterns in the vessels that supply the liver, the intestine, and other abdominal organs. A combination of increased pressure and local inflammation may lead to PLE. Many different medical therapies have been tried for patients with PLE following the Fontan procedure. None have been found to be universally successful. In addition to different medications, dietary changes are often advised including consumption of a high-protein, low-fat diet. In patients with severe PLE who are non-responsive to medical therapy or dietary changes, heart transplantation may be successful in resolving the PLE."

Chapter 11

LIVING FOR EDEN

PART 6

JANUARY 17, 2009

Do I Miss My Day Job?

People keep asking me if I miss my day job. No, I don't. At least I haven't until today.

I play the piano, and I run a small independent record label called Stone Angel Music. In addition to my own piano music, our artists like Steven Sharp Nelson mostly record peaceful instrumental albums. The music we produce has been a major part of my life.

But last fall when my health began failing and doctors listed me for the transplant, I canceled over twenty gigs, and I stopped spending time promoting music.

That's been the difficult part. I miss playing for people. And more particularly, I miss sharing my life's philosophy in a concert or fireside setting.

I think I've been blessed not to really think about it.

The music is still within me.

I guess it's the drama of the unknown and the fact that all I can think about is my wife and little girl. I want more time with them, and I don't want anything to get in the way.

I look forward to recovering from the challenging surgery. It will be a difficult road for many months. But I wouldn't trade this experience for anything. I am learning a great deal about life and its purpose, and I've come to understand the character of my family, friends, and other associates.

I'm getting anxious. I want to do so much in this life and give back to those who've selflessly served and sacrificed their time for my family and me.

And, yes, I have music in me. It's building up. I can feel it. Hopefully, with faith, prayers, and the incredible medical team, I'll get another chance to let it out.

Chapter 12

THE GIFT OF MUSIC

There were no musicians in our home growing up except for me and my brother Brian, who picked up a guitar and began writing and singing his own music. My sisters and I took piano lessons from my great-aunt Muriel. She taught us how to play on her old upright piano in her basement, and she held occasional recitals for students and their families. I remember as an eight-year-old going into her food-storage room that had cold concrete floors to select sheet music from her various cabinets.

My first and last recital piece under Muriel was a sloppy version of the theme to a popular soda commercial from the 1980s. The song was called "Coke Is It!" Of course, I lasted less than a year in piano lessons because my lack of desire to practice, according to my mother and Muriel. In fact, my piano teacher said that I was a "frustrating student to teach."

When I turned twelve, I started playing the cello, but that lasted less than six months because I hated carrying the large instrument home from school each day. Besides, I thought I looked silly carrying it. So between the recorder that kids dabble with in elementary school, less than a year of piano, and a bit of practice on a cello bigger than me, I had no music in me until high school (other than a love for popular songs on the radio).

As a twelve-year-old sharing a room with younger brothers, I put an old FM transistor radio under my pillow at night so I could hear the "Top 10 at 10:00" on the local rock station. It was during this time that my father kindly questioned why I was spending all of my earnings from an early-morning paper route on records and cassettes from the local music store.

One day during my junior year of high school, I was walking down a hallway during class and I heard a piano melody. Like in the story of the Pied Piper, I followed the music. In the auditorium, behind the stage near the loading docks, I found senior Ryan Stewart playing on a large, black grand Steinway piano. He said, "Come in and sit down."

I sat and listened intensely as I watched his fingers fly all over the keyboard, playing notes as though he hadn't even touched them. I couldn't understand how Ryan was able to move his fingers so quickly up and down the piano.

Ryan's music was beautiful. Not classical. Not jazz. His music was more like a soundtrack to experiences in life, like taking the melodies of the Beatles and mixing them with Mozart. I learned he was improvising the popular "new age" music of our time, playing songs by Mannheim Steamroller, David Lanz, Yanni, and George Winston.

I said to Ryan, "I'm messing around with a few melodies but I don't have the gift you have." He didn't seem concerned, so I continued, "I can do a few things in my right hand but I have no idea how to incorporate my left hand." He said, "I'm late for class. Come to my home after school and I'll show you what to do."

After school, I went to the Stewart house, which was a couple blocks from my home. The door was wide open and, just like in the school hallway, I followed the music to a room located by the back porch, next to the kitchen. There Ryan sat at another beautiful, black grand Steinway.

People were coming and going in the Stewart home. As he continued playing David Lanz's "Return to the Heart," Ryan motioned me to come in and said, "Sit here by me." I sat on the piano bench listening and watching his every move with great interest. He showed me a flowing motion in the left hand he called *arpeggio* (Italian for "broken chords"), where the notes are played in sequence, one after the other, rather than ringing out in unison.

As I sat trying to apply this technique, I noticed that two teenage girls kept coming in and out of the room to see what was going on. Ryan said, "Ignore them. That's my little sister Lynnette and her friend Luci."

Over the next several months, I tried to apply the lesson Ryan shared with me. I was determined to learn to play the piano, but I was missing the talent needed to play the instrument with the same elegance, grace, and passion that I admired in professionals.

As the leaves began to fall in 1991, a spiritual gift of music fell upon me after I experienced deep heartache. It came like lightning as I was trying to understand the death of close friend.

Dave Creer had a gifted wit, a dry sense of humor, loved the piano man Billy Joel, imitated talk show host David Letterman, and enjoyed racing his Red Berretta down a hill we called "the gully" on the way home from school each day.

The phone call came while I was listening to a girlfriend practice Chopin for a piano performance competition. On the line was my friend and student leader Paul Mayfield. He explained that about an hour earlier, my friend Dave had died in a tragic auto-pedestrian accident.

I was shocked. I could not wrap my mind around Dave's death. Not only had I seen him earlier that morning, but I was unfamiliar with tragedy. Most people I had known either grew old or had a lasting disease. Except for the funeral of my childhood friend Andrew, the funerals I had gone to were fairly joyous occasions attended by hundreds of family members and friends, all celebrating the long, fulfilled life of the person who had passed.

However, the sudden death of a good friend—a young friend—was challenging, and with it began a period of growth and understanding for me. Because of my health problem with its various critical surgeries and near-death experiences, I felt the fragile nature of life, and it bothered me.

Rehearsing for a show in a small town Maryland Theater.

I wondered, Why is a healthy and vibrant person like Dave suddenly taken from this life into the next? I questioned God: Dave had more energy than me and would be far more effective here than I will, why wasn't I the one taken home? I felt what some might call survivor's guilt.

Over the next several weeks before I went to bed, I knelt in prayer and asked God for help and understanding. In the quiet afternoons when school was over, I sat in my parents' living room at our family piano, an old upright Kawai.

One day, a quiet miracle occurred. I gently touched one key here and another there. With each key came a tone from the piano that seemed to pierce my soul. I felt something powerful and healing flow into me. When I played a scale of keys like climbing steps, or mixed up each of them one at a time, I heard something divine speak to my soul. It was as if music had opened a conduit to heaven, and suddenly I found peace and comfort to cope with losing my friend.

Over the next several months, I spent hours each day perfecting all I had been taught and given. However imperfect it was, music had become the medium that would change my life, heal my soul, and allow me to express myself spiritually.

My senior year our school held its annual Concerto Night featuring students performing classical works on violin, cello, piano, and other instruments. My new friend Ryan Stewart had entered his own piece the year before and had been chosen to perform with the high school orchestra that year. He said to me, "You should do this."

Intimidated and confused, I replied, "I can't write a concerto."

"Yes, you can, and I'll help you," he insisted. By ear, I composed what probably sounded like Russian polka meets a Nintendo game soundtrack. Ryan transcribed the music to paper, and we handed the "masterpiece" into Jack Ashton, our school conductor and a member of the prestigious Utah Symphony on a Friday. On Monday I learned from Mr. Ashton that the piece was accepted, but on condition that we would have the piece orchestrated by the following Monday. "Sure, we can do that," I said with some hesitation. Worried, I found Ryan and told him we needed orchestration. "Let's do it this weekend," he said nonchalantly.

With a couple of boxes of Twinkies and some six-packs of

soda, Ryan and I stayed up late over the weekend and composed the orchestral parts for the piano concerto. For such a young person, Ryan's musical abilities were remarkable.

The piece was accepted and I practiced for Concerto Night. We held one rehearsal with the orchestra and, although the kids squinted at our copied notation through thick-rimmed glasses, you could tell there was a song somewhere in all of the noise of squeaking bows, laughter, and coughing.

For Concerto Night, the program listed the various composers whose works would be featured that evening—names such as Mozart, Beethoven, Bach, Chopin, and Cardall. We laughed at the last name. Having heard my own concerto, I knew that had the other composers been alive, they would have been truly insulted. Nevertheless, my experience performing a concerto live with a full orchestra in front of a large crowd was breathtaking. I had never felt so nervous and so alive. I knew I wanted more of this.

After graduation, I took a job playing my solo piano music in a restaurant. I never would have imagined that someone would pay me to play the piano; and on top of that, people actually gave me tips. This was like getting paid to play professional football. I was excited and thrilled for the opportunity.

As I kept performing and as people responded positively, my desire was fueled to somehow make a career out of playing the piano. I began learning everything I could about the music industry.

I recall words of Howard W. Hunter, who served as president of The Church of Jesus Christ of Latter-day Saints. My father was fortunate to interview this spiritual giant when President Hunter was in his eighties, and Dad asked him about the music President Hunter had performed when he was young.

As a teenager, President Hunter became proficient on as many as ten musical instruments, and he later created a successful jazz five-piece combo called Hunter's Croonaders, which toured the Orient and became quite popular. "We did dance music, dinner music, and classical," said President Hunter.

My father asked, "Did you ever consider making music your career?"

President Hunter replied, "Not really. I was playing in a ballroom in Los Angeles until the Saturday night before we were married." He continued, "On that night, after the ballroom engagement, I took all my instruments and wrapped them up and put them in their cases. Some of them are still wrapped up. I decided that was the end."

"Why did you feel to make that decision at that point?" asked my father.

Then came the response that has stayed in my mind and heart. President Hunter said, "Because of the association. Musicians have rather a poor record as far as morality, drinking, drugs, and a lot of others things . . . and I just thought there was a better life than that . . . and so I just cut it off short and sharp and we went to the temple and were married."

I decided early I would never let music take precedence over things that really mattered. My family and God would always come first. Music would be an occupation with a means to an end, a tool or an instrument, to spread goodness in the world. Through my music I would try to offer hope and healing to those who are troubled, and peace to those seeking refuge from life's daily grind.

Chapter 13

LIVING FOR EDEN

PART 7

JANUARY 21, 2009

Moving into the Hospital

I am moving permanently into the hospital on Monday until doctors can get me a heart and I'm recovered. WILD! They'll also up my status, putting me at the top of the waiting list.

JANUARY 22, 2009

False Alarm! Staying Home

False alarm. I apologize for crying wolf again, but I'm not moving into the hospital on Monday after all. We met with doctors today, and apparently my body is no longer anemic and my protein levels have improved. We did not think that would happen. However, two weeks ago I was infused over a five-day period with iron to help improve my blood and give me strength. So this wonderful miracle is great news!

But it is temporary good news, and I may yet again find myself in the hospital with more challenges. You mentally prepare yourself for something, and then things change. Life is unpredictable, but it keeps moving along for all of us. I love it! And although I have anxieties with waiting for a heart, I am truly blessed and grateful for the gift of life.

I am feeling good, so I'll just enjoy this time. But what a roller coaster!

JANUARY 29, 2009
What Is It That You Think About?

A close friend of mine asked me, "With your situation, what is it that you think about?" That is a good question. When you're waiting for an event to happen that could determine your fate, what do you think about? For me, it's a chance to take a look back at life and reflect on events and who I've become and where I'm headed.

What consumes my mind is what matters most to me: my playful little three-year-old daughter, Eden, and my angel of a wife, Lynnette.

It's so unfortunate that millions of men don't know what I am talking about. When asked about his newfound family life and fatherhood, comedian Jerry Seinfeld, who lived many

Taking Eden to her first movie.

years as a bachelor, said, "I love being married . . . I would never want to be married to anyone else, . . . I love my wife."[1]

FEBRUARY 6, 2009

Getting Out

Yesterday at the clinic, my transplant cardiologist, Melanie Everitt, said my lab work looked good. I have more color in my face because I am no longer anemic, thanks to iron

*Lynnette, Eden, and I visiting the historic Tabernacle on Temple
Square in our hometown of Salt Lake City, Utah.*

infusions. I am also feeling better than I have been, given the
circumstances.

I was able to take my family on a few outings this past
week, which we haven't done in a long time. We visited
downtown Salt Lake City and saw some historical sites, including the Salt Lake Tabernacle on Temple Square. We also
had some good friends take us to dinner for big, juicy steaks.
I am eating like 100 grams of protein each day with the hope
I'll absorb some of it.

This is all good news! I need to be strong for the transplant operation, because it will help in the long recovery.

I am fortunate to be in the care of wonderful doctors and

nurses. I feel a great connection with each one of them, and I trust their judgment.

Every time I go into the Primary Children's Medical Center to receive care, I see kids in hard circumstances. Still, I'm at peace knowing a few of the people who are providing their medical care.

We did learn that my heart is having premature ventricular contraction (PVC), also known as ventricular premature beat (VPB) or extrasystole. It's a form of irregular heartbeats in which the ventricle contracts prematurely. This may be perceived as a "skipped beat" or as palpitations. So for the past twenty-four hours my heart has been monitored to see how often I have them.

Possible triggers of PVC (I commented on each of these):
• Anxiety/Stress (I have some of this)
• Chocolate (I do eat a lot of this)
• Caffeine (Coca-Cola, yes)
• Cocaine or other stimulant (No)
• Calcium/magnesium imbalance (Yes, I have this)
• Dehydration (sometimes)
• Exercise (I don't do this)
• Hormonal imbalance (Nope)
• Hypercapnia (C02 poisoning) (I have no idea)
• Hyperstimulation of the Vagus nerve (Not sure)
• Lack of sleep/exhaustion (Yes, this is true)
• Overeating (A little bit)
• Low copper (I don't eat pennies!)
• MSG (I think this is in a bunch of the food I eat)

FEBRUARY 12, 2009

Say a Prayer This Valentine's for the Cardiac Kids

In the past six months since I was listed for a new heart, my wife and I have read other related blogs. It's sobering to see so many "cardiac kids," or children with congenital heart disease. Some of these sweet souls have had transplants. Others are waiting. There have been miracles, struggles, and loss of life.

It's inspiring to interact with a few of these families. I'm sure several share my medical team at Primary Children's Medical Center. It's a wonderful staff of experts who are passionate in their work to save lives. But more important to me, the cardiology and transplant staffs have a peaceful, caring spirit about them.

Although I am aware of the many adults in my same shoes, I would hope they'd agree with me when I say that living thirty-five years is a great blessing and an honor. I hope to have many more years. I have a daughter who needs a father. But my heart is crying out for these "cardiac kids," that they might have a chance to enjoy this beautiful world. Just as badly as I want to live for my daughter, I want these sons and daughters to live for their parents.

Several months ago, while I was staying in the hospital with my health declining, I remember being discouraged with life and my situation. And although I struggled mentally, I said a quiet prayer. Moments later, I recalled something I heard from a man I greatly admire. He said, "Despair drains from us all that is vibrant and joyful and leaves behind the empty remnants of what life was meant to be. Despair kills ambition, advances sickness, pollutes the soul, and deadens the heart. Despair can seem like a staircase that leads only and forever downward.

"Hope, on the other hand, is like the beam of sunlight rising up and above the horizon of our present circumstances. It pierces the darkness with a brilliant dawn."[2] Upon remembering this message, I regained my optimism and felt peace again.

This Valentine's weekend, as we think of hearts, I invite you to join with me in remembering these "cardiac kids" and their families. Say a prayer for them.

FEBRUARY 18, 2009
Bone Transfusions

Milk won't cut it. My calcium is low. It's an 8. Should be 8.7, but that's all right because nobody is perfect. Nonetheless, I had my second transfusion to strengthen my bones. My last one was three months ago. You basically get hooked up to another IV, lie on a bed, listen to some tunes, and wait three hours. I listened to some Jack Johnson, a little Journey, and a sermon by Dieter F. Uchtdorf. Oh, you do get a drink. They gave me BOOST. And a turkey sandwich (like the ones they have on Delta Airlines when you sit in coach). That was thoughtful.

Tomorrow I get to have some more labs drawn and see doctors Yetman and Everitt. They're brilliant women, and so are the many good folks that work with them to save so many lives.

Heart to Heart

My doctors said my health is stable, which is good since transplants are down 29 percent in the region. It's going to take some time. As long as I'm feeling some strength, I don't mind waiting. But when I don't feel good, I'm hoping the surgery won't be too far off. Nevertheless, life is wonderful. My wife and daughter are angels and I love each day with them! My extended family is incredibly supportive and has sacrificed much in our behalf. I'm constantly in awe of the goodness of God and His rich blessings that pour down upon us.

I should admit, though, that with all of the medications I'm taking, including my shots and internal IV, I get anxious. I have to stay busy even though I'm extremely tired and am usually just sitting around. You should know, for those of you at work or trying to keep up with kids, there is no good television during the day, and all the new movies Hollywood produces make me feel like I'm wasting precious time. So I have found great happiness doing many other things. When I'm not being entertained by Eden or enjoying conversation with Lynnette, I'm doing quite a bit of reading, listening to music

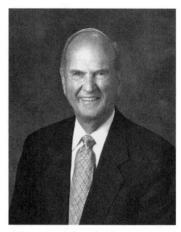

Russell M. Nelson, former cardiovascular thoracic surgeon and currently an ecclesiastical leader in The Church of Jesus Christ of Latter-day Saints.

or great speeches and sermons, answering e-mails, writing notes, running my small record label, and blogging, which I am now addicted to, having just created another blog—http://hope4things.blogspot.com.

I've been deeply inspired reading the autobiography *From Heart to Heart,* by one of my spiritual heroes, Russell M. Nelson. He is a great leader, teacher, and Apostle in The Church of Jesus Christ of Latter-day Saints. Before he became an Apostle, he was a heart surgeon. He's world renowned for his contribution in helping a team of interns and doctors create the first artificial heart-lung machine (cardiopulmonary bypass), which makes open-heart surgery possible. This machine made it possible for blood to bypass my heart in order for surgeons to remove my endocarditis in 1986, and to allow me to receive the Fontan procedure in 1987. This amazing machine will be a major part of my heart transplant and has saved millions of lives.

In *From Heart to Heart,* there is a beautiful description of the body and how it works. Russell M. Nelson speaks about the heart and how powerful it is. "The heart has four little valves that open and close more than 100,000 times a day, over 36 million times a year. There is no material yet devised by man capable of flexing that many times without ultimate fatigue and fracture. The best artificial heart valve available to us now is that taken from the lowly pig. . . . To date, it is better than any of the valves man has made from steel and plastic, although we don't know yet how durable it may be.

"The amount of work done by the heart is most amazing. Each day it pumps enough fluid to fill a 2,000-gallon tank car and performs work equivalent to lifting a 150-pound man to the top of the Empire State Building, while consuming about four watts, less energy than is used by the smallest light bulb in our home.

"At the crest of the heart is a little electrical transmitter, the sinoatrial node, which sends its signal over the network of special conduction tissue throughout the heart to organize the heartbeat and synchronize it in response to the extra demands of exercise and the lessened demands at rest.

". . . Thousands of doctors . . . [are] probing deeply to learn more about this simple pump. It seems that the more we learn, the more we have yet to learn."[3]

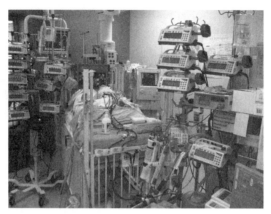

The various machines and computers used by medical personnel fighting to preserve the lives of infants such as Gracie Gledhill who have unique heart anatomy.

FEBRUARY 23, 2009

Say a Prayer for Gracie

I have been deeply affected by a little girl named Gracie Gledhill. It has been up-and-down for her sweet family, whom I've never met. I heard about her from a woman who lost her child to CHD (congenital heart disease). Immediately, I was drawn to Gracie's story. Her mother, father, two brothers, one sister, and a countless number of other people have been praying for this little girl. Gracie was born with a severe congenital heart disease. After various uphill battles, hope, and prayer, she was listed for a heart last Tuesday. She was placed at the top of the list under the care of my transplant physician. I witnessed a miracle when I learned Saturday night that a call came. Doctors had a heart for Gracie. Throughout the night, morning, afternoon, and into the evening, her mother updated her blog whenever they had news. I kept checking in to see what was happening.

But today she is struggling to survive because her body is rejecting the heart. I don't know what's going to happen. But I am humbled. This is a sobering experience. A great man once wrote something like, "I don't know the meaning of all things but I know that God loves his children."

Say a prayer for the Gracie Gledhill family.

FEBRUARY 27, 2009
Life Is a Great Gift!

I have been richly blessed as I continue to wait for a heart. This journey has been nothing short of a miracle. Life is a great gift, and I look forward to each new day.

I want to thank all of you for your thoughts and prayers on behalf of my little family.

My new blog friends are wonderful! Thank you for sharing your lives with me. All your comments have given me great strength. Please forgive me if I am not able to respond.

I want to thank Lynnette—for everything. She doesn't have much time to herself these days. When she's not working as an RN in the IMC newborn intensive care unit, she is caring for our daughter. Lynnette has been the great blessing of my life. In dealing day to day with my health issues

Our last family portrait while waiting for a heart transplant.

and my unforeseen future, she is a saint. I married my best friend, and I ache to spend every waking moment with her. I adore her love, patience, loyalty, spirituality, humor, wisdom, and beauty. Our sweet little girl, Eden, continues to laugh, dance, and learn how much love we have for each other through all these ups and downs.

I want to thank my parents for setting me loose as a child and allowing my heart and lungs to strengthen whenever I had a heart surgery. God put me in their arms.

I have a lot of siblings and siblings-in-law. There are so many it would take a whole page to mention each one. Each is amazing and a great example to me. My daughter adores her cousins. Everyone has thrown their arms around us in this time and has been available to help at a wink's notice. I love you guys!

My friends and those who I attend church with have

been a wonderful blessing, and I look forward to seeing their faces each Sunday and throughout the week for various reasons. I love being involved and helping where I can. Now that I'm on the receiving end of acts of service, I deeply appreciate what they do.

And I want to thank the wonderful medical team at Primary Children's Medical Center. I have been blessed over the years with great cardiologists, nurses, radiologists, etc. The list is too long to mention. I've enjoyed care from experts at Intermountain Medical Center, The University of Utah Hospital, Jordan Valley hospital, and Primary Children's Medical Center. Of these great folks, I want to especially recognize Doctors "Uncle" George Veasy, Conrad Jensen, Donald Doty, John Hawkins, Dale Renlund, Abdallah Kfoury, Patrick Fisher, Larry Green, Michael Adjei Poku, Ed Clark, Charles King, Peter Kouretas, Aditya Kaza, Ronald Day, Robert Gray, Elizabeth Saarel, Susan Etheridge, Roger Freedman, Brian Crandall, John Doty, and the many others who've worked on my case.

I am blessed at this time to consult with adult congenital heart doctor Angela Yetman. She is a fighter and very optimistic. She is extremely intelligent, and my wife and I greatly admire her.

I have a wonderful transplant cardiologist, Melanie Everitt, along with her team: Michelle Cardon, Emily Bullock, and others. They are always upbeat and I look forward to seeing them each visit. Those who've worked with

Gracie Jean Gledhill (March 20, 2008–March 2, 2009).

Dr. Everitt will agree that her sensitivity and caring nature is an absolute bonus to her wisdom.

Overall, thank you, everyone! I love life. I am determined. You have all strengthened my conviction to carry on.

MARCH 3, 2009

Gracie Passed Away Last Night

Gracie Gledhill passed away last night. She was born a year ago with hypoplastic left heart syndrome (HLHS). Gracie had her first surgery, the Norwood, when she was four days old. She was scheduled for her second surgery, the Glenn, on February 12, 2009, but it was determined that her heart was too sick and the surgery would be too risky. Gracie needed a heart transplant to live. A heart became available after she was on the transplant list just three days, and she had a heart transplant on February 22, 2009. Unfortunately, the heart didn't take, and she came out of surgery on life support (ECMO). Yesterday, she was taken off life support, and she gradually slipped away.

For a short season Gracie influenced a lot of people. My wife and I have shed many tears for this child, her siblings, and parents, whom we've never met personally. But we share the same doctors, the same hospital, and the same religious beliefs, and we have corresponded through e-mail. Incidentally, my wife and I have always loved the name Gracie, and we had planned to give that name to a daughter we miscarried (our fifth miscarriage).

Anyone who reads the Gledhills' journey of ups and downs in dealing with Gracie's congenital heart disease will feel a closeness or connection with her, because all of us are dealing in some way or another with life and its challenges. Gracie left behind her brothers, Max and Taylor; her sister, Callie; her mother, Michele; and her father, Tom.

Over the years, I have been deeply affected by other sick children I've associated with while staying at Primary Children's. It's heartbreaking to know parents and medical personnel who've fought to keep children alive only to see them slowly slip away back into God's loving arms. And it's inspiring to witness children who've been fortunate to continue their journey in this life. I am one of those. Regardless of the outcome, it seems that these lives teach all of us the

Meeting Gracie's parents, Tom and Michele Gledhill, at Gracie's funeral.

value of our own lives and how fragile we are. We live for a short while, but in the end we all go home to that God who gave us life. Some of us just get to go a little earlier than we expected.

MARCH 9, 2009

The Living for Eden Benefit Concert

My family and I are very grateful for all of the support we're receiving from our community. I have great friends and colleagues in the music industry whom I greatly admire. I learned a couple of days ago that a few of them—Kurt Bestor, Peter Breinholt, Ryan Shupe & the Rubberband, Sam Payne, and some others—are coming together to do a benefit concert for our family. They're calling the evening "Living for Eden."

All I can say is, thank you! I hope to go and see many of you there, unless of course, I happen to get a call for a heart. That would also be nice.

MARCH 11, 2009
Gracie and My Daily Routine

I mentioned in a previous blog that Gracie Gledhill passed away almost a week after her eleven-month-old body rejected her heart transplant. Even before she passed, I was invited by her kind grandfather to consider playing the piano at Gracie's funeral. I told him, "I would much rather see Gracie in her mother's arms at one of my shows, after I also recover from a transplant, than to see her at her funeral." But it wasn't meant to be, and I am extremely humbled and honored to have participated in one of the most touching funerals I've ever attended. My wife and I will never forget it. Michele's blog for her daughter has strengthened my love of life and God.

MY ROUTINE

Two hundred days seems like a long time, but the time has flown by. I am feeling good. I've got a routine down. When I'm not seeing the doctor or going to church, I usually get up between eight and nine in the morning to the sound of my daughter wanting to watch "a show." I take my first dose of meds and drink a lot of water. I read the news online, and at ten o'clock I give myself a shot and take more meds. We make breakfast. I answer some e-mails. On a good day a friend takes me to lunch. I come home and take more meds. I lay down and listen to a talk or sermon, read a little bit, get online, and try to play with Eden. Around five o'clock I help my wife make dinner, try to answer some phone calls, answer some e-mails, and listen to music while Eden dances around the house. I take my final meds. I give myself another shot, read a little bit more, blog, listen to music or a talk, and go to bed.

In the News

My good friends at Intermountain Donor Services in Salt Lake City have been asking me to share my story with our community through the media. It took a while before I said yes. But I changed my mind because of the number of parents I've observed with children who are affected by congenital heart disease (CHD).

My parents have never given up on me, and I now have my own family. Even to this day they stay positive, and that motivates me. It's inspiring. It doesn't mean we haven't had our share of tears and frustrations. But they've kept an optimistic attitude about life. They keep hope alive. As Dieter F.

Waiting to have my blood drawn for lab results at Primary Children's Medical Center, a weekly occurrence. Lynnette is playing with Eden in the background.

Uchtdorf stated, "Each time a hope is fulfilled, it creates confidence and leads to greater hope."[4]

I've said this many times, but I'm extremely blessed to have lived almost thirty-six years after doctors thought I wouldn't make it. If there is one thing I've learned, it is that we are not in charge. There is a finale for each of us. Those around us are subject to that. But until then, we all do our best to fight to survive either for ourselves or for our children. It's mind over matter. I have no doubt that there is something greater than all of this guiding our lives, the lives of our children, and the world in which we experience life.

Another hero of mine, Gordon B. Hinckley, said, and I now understand the humor of what he meant, "You go to bed each night and you be sure to get up in the morning."[5]

I hope in sharing my story it might help your life in some way. We are all trying to find joy in the journey. These experiences allow each of us to understand the full measure of that word *joy*. But joy does not come into our hearts until we have experienced a lot of pain, heartache, and tears. As C. S. Lewis said, "God whispers to us in our pleasures, speaks in our conscience, but shouts in our pain; it is His megaphone to rouse a deaf world."[6]

MARCH 20, 2009

And What of Dying?

Thoughts of the future are heavy on my mind. I should note that I am at peace. My faith sustains me. But it's impossible for me not to discuss feelings on the subject of dying—living in my shoes with heart failure that requires a transplant, and not just any transplant, but a rather difficult surgery requiring several pediatric thoracic surgeons.

I sometimes think most of us are in denial about growing old and eventually facing our own death. Everyone dies. We accept birth and love to talk to about it, but what of dying?

As a child you don't think or talk about your own death because you just got here. As adults it's a taboo subject and doesn't always make for delightful conversation with friends. But living with a disease, you are reminded all of the time that you probably won't grow old.

At age thirteen when I lay deathly ill with endocarditis

in the hospital, I had no notion that I could die during that time. I thought to myself, "I'll be fine." Of course, we all know kids believe they are immortal, especially teenagers.

As an adult it becomes much more difficult to think about. I have responsibility. I'm a father and husband. The truth is I am not afraid to die because my faith sustains me, but I am afraid of missing out on my daughter's life and helping my wife raise her.

The beauty in suffering and sharing it with Lynnette is that our comprehension of our love and affection for each other stays on the surface and becomes what I consider the most valuable and important time of our marriage. We hold each other closer because of what could happen and the nostalgia we feel.

I don't wish dying on anyone. But if we could think about our own death for two or three minutes each day, I believe we would see the world differently. If we thought of what life would be like without that certain someone, how would we treat him or her? The argument we had with a friend or family member becomes meaningless. The world in general becomes more beautiful. Each day is a new gift from God. Life becomes a greater opportunity to do something positive to make this world better. In the movie *Braveheart,* Mel Gibson (as William Wallace) says, "Every man dies. Not every man really lives."[7]

I don't know what will happen to me, but I certainly love each moment I have and look forward to each waking day. I do think the longer you wait for a transplant, the longer you have to think, speculate, and wonder.

My cardiologists have brilliantly stabilized my health and prepared me for the challenging surgery. I'm confident in my thoracic surgeons and the great team they work with. They are skilled professionals, and I have deep respect for their work. Fortunately, they've had time to review my case over these past seven months.

Ultimately, I believe that I am in the hands of a loving God whom I've asked humbly to allow me more time in this world to enjoy its beauty and people.

MARCH 24, 2009
Forget Yourself and Go to Work

Snow fell yesterday. I have a comfortable chair that reclines next to our bedroom window so I can look outside while I work, read, sleep, or watch television. As I sat in my chair, I heard the scraping of a snow shovel on our driveway and looked out to see a friend, whom I have not seen in months, out shoveling our snow. I called him this morning and I learned he was out of work. And yet what did he choose to do yesterday instead of feeling sorry for himself in his jobless situation? He got up, put on a coat, grabbed his shovel, and served another.

This friend is one example of many who have selflessly given of their time and talents to bless the lives of another

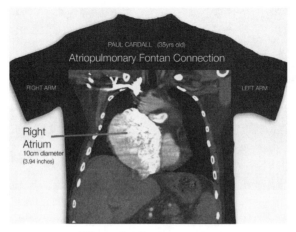

CT scan of my Fontan connection.

even though their own circumstances are dire. Albert Einstein wrote, "Only a life lived for others is a life worthwhile."[8] And Mahatma Gandhi declared, "The best way to find yourself is to lose yourself in the service of others."[9]

I'm grateful to the Baron Music Group, who gathered many of my colleagues and friends for a benefit concert in behalf of our family called "Living for Eden." Our friends Kurt Bestor, Peter Breinholt, Ryan Shupe & the Rubberband, Colors, and Sam Payne are all incredible artists and musicians who normally get paid to perform, so we are truly humbled. Several of them spent last week in Bulgaria performing for some orphanages, and yet they came home to do even more service, this time for me. I can tell you that if these guys were selling cars they'd probably make a fortune.

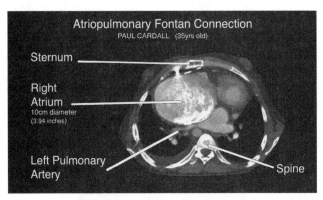

This image, taken before the stent placement, shows the left pulmonary artery being squished by the right atrium. (The spine is on the bottom and the chest wall is on the top. The lungs are black and the ribs are white.)

Yet they choose to uplift and inspire through the power of music.

In my own situation and through the years, if I've learned anything about life, it is that in order to have true and lasting happiness (which is joy), you can't wallow in your own suffering or poverty. You must empower yourself to reach out to those with much greater need. When Gordon B. Hinckley faced a period of discouragement as a young man, his father advised him, "Forget yourself and go to work."[10] Neal A. Maxwell stated, "God does not begin by asking us about our ability, but only about our availability, and if we then prove our dependability, he will increase our capability."[11]

MARCH 27, 2009

What's Up, Doc?

I went to the transplant clinic today to meet with Doctor Everitt and Doctor Yetman. I also ran into one of my thoracic surgeons, Dr. Peter Kouretas. They are a wonderful team, and I enjoy seeing them. The highlight of the clinic for my wife and me was interacting with a few of the "heart moms" and their beautiful children who've been "transplanted." We saw little Daxton, pretty Kaidence, and baby Benjamin.

I went home feeling extremely confident about the actual transplant surgery. Doctor Yetman said that transplants are one of the easier forms of heart surgery, although my anatomy will make it a little more challenging. It's the recovery that will be the most difficult time, according to doctors. I remember that Dr. Kouretas' colleague Dr. Hawkins assured me that there is an 80 percent chance they'll need to reopen my chest to get rid of excess fluid. I say, "Just put a zipper on there and go to town."

Adults who've had the Fontan procedure, like I have, apparently recover much more slowly. I could be in the hospital two to three months. Nobody really knows. I told them that for that time period, just bring me some hospital Jell-O through a straw and turn on some good music. As long as I get an opportunity to go home and enjoy my little girl and wonderful wife, I am ready to run that marathon until I reach that finish, no matter how hard it will be.

*Backstage at the Living for Eden Benefit Concert
(Ryan Shupe, Tom Gledhill, Paul Cardall, Kurt Bestor,
Michele Gledhill and children Max, Callie, and Taylor).*

APRIL 7, 2009

The Living for Eden Concert

Words cannot adequately express our sincere appreciation to all of you for joining with us to celebrate life and "Living for Eden" last evening at the 3,000-seat auditorium at Cottonwood High School in Utah. At the benefit concert given for us, our family experienced a feeling of love that we will cherish for a very long time. You are wonderful, and we will never forget your kindness, love, and support.

We are optimistic about my future! And whether things go as we hope or not, one thing I do know is that every day we have to enjoy life should be celebrated. It is a gift from our Heavenly Father. We live in a beautiful world, and I look forward to each new day.

Finally, a special thank you to all of the musicians, producers, ushers, volunteers, family, and friends, and the two people who pulled their resources together to do this event—my good friend and former business partner Jeremy Baron of the Baron Music Group, and my dear sister Carol Burgoyne, who is not only one of my best friends but one of the most talented organizers I know.

Thank you, everyone. We love you!

Paul, Lynnette, & Eden

In addition, please say a prayer for baby Jack, who is going in tomorrow morning for his Fontan procedure at Primary Children's Medical Center. And pray for Dr. Peter Kouretas, who will perform the delicate procedure. The Fontan that I received was the old version, and it has sustained my life for twenty-two years. The new Fontan will go much further and longer for kids like Jack. Also, baby boy Grant (HLHS) is going to have some surgery. Say a prayer for him. http://grantmeaheart.blogspot.com/.

APRIL 10, 2009

Clinic Update and a Story from the Concert

My bimonthly clinic concluded that my health is stable. Isn't it nice to be told you're clinically stable? I have more color in my

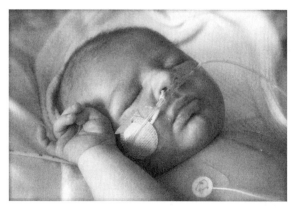

Baby Grant Hicken after his heart surgery.

face. I'm producing more red blood cells. (This could explain my leaning toward college-blue BYU all of these years.) On Tuesday, I will undergo a heart cath or cardiac catheterization.

We continue to get feedback from the concert and are hearing wonderful stories about people who attended the show. My wife and I are still humbled by the outpouring of love and support!

This e-mail came from Kyle and Allie, the parents of my fellow cardiac pal Grant, who is recovering from some challenging surgery.

"Last night, we had another huge blessing. We have wanted to attend a benefit concert for Paul Cardall (a musician who has a heart defect similar to Grant and who is waiting for his heart transplant), but we were unsure of where life would take us and so we did not buy tickets.

"Yesterday, after we decided we trusted our nurses for the day and we knew our night nurse, we decided we could attempt our first real outing away from the hospital! To our dismay, tickets were sold out. We started trying to find some tickets and just after posting and e-mailing a few people, someone came on the intercom here and announced that they had tickets for the concert that they were not using that they wanted to donate to a family here on the floor. What a fast answer to a simple hopeful prayer! We claimed the tickets and were able to go with a few friends last night.

"What a wonderful concert it was. I had major anxiety leaving Grant for so long, but it was good to be there. We met many heart families whom we had previously known only through the world of blogs and thoroughly enjoyed the entertainment. Paul was able to stand with his family and thank those in attendance for their support and it was wonderful to see him, though weak, still full of hope.

"There was a beautiful tribute to Gracie Gledhill and recognition of the many other families with "cardiac kids" and the whole heart community was there to embrace one another. We spoke with Tom and Michele Gledhill right before the concert, and I was so glad for their family to continue to see little Gracie living on and touching lives—just as each of these sweet angel babies do to all who know them and their lives.

"I loved being there, but I was glad to be back with my sweet baby."

There are a lot of cardiac kids who are in need of help,

and there are mothers with empty arms—mothers who need our prayers. When you retire this evening, remember them, and don't forget to say a prayer for Grant and his family.

My Heart Cath

Prior to yesterday's heart cath, Lynnette and I were fortunate to visit with little Grant and his parents, Kyle and Allie. Grant was born with HLHS and needed some repair work on his liver. But gratefully, after many prayers and good medical care, Grant is on the mend and doing better. Doctors need to keep him in the pediatric intensive care unit (PICU) for another couple of weeks before Kyle and Allie can take him home. In the meantime, his parents have an RV they can stay in parked at the hospital. Kyle has been attending school in Logan, Utah.

While in the PICU, we saw many familiar faces and had a brief conversation with one of my surgeons. We also learned that little Jack is recovering very well from his Fontan, and they hope to take him home soon.

As for my cath, we checked in at noon and waited with other same-day-surgery children. I always enjoy sitting there as the only adult going into a procedure. Toys are everywhere. There was one woman telling her grandson how to play his video game. So I pulled out my iPhone and played a golf game.

We were called into a room after thirty minutes. They checked my vital stats and had me put on a gown. Doctor Gray came in and we discussed the procedure, which would be my third cath since being listed for a heart last August.

My anesthesiologist came into the room and we discussed how they wouldn't put me completely under like the children, but they would give me an anti-anxiety drug and another to cause amnesia. (In my childhood I remember being awake for most of these caths, although they now put the kids completely out.)

After saying good-bye to Lynnette, I walked into the cath lab, which looks like an operation room. There were several nurses and techs prepping the room. We joked about the tempurpedic mattress on the narrow operating table. We laughed about many other things as I lay flat on the table.

They hooked me up to machines and began a slow drip of the drug into a new IV in my left hand. My 24/7 medication, Milrinone, was still running into my PICC. I continued joking about my vulnerable situation. The radio was playing "Round and Round" by a metal band called RATT. I hadn't heard that song in a long time. I mentioned, "You're putting me out to this '80s song?" Slowly, I faded or drifted off, and the procedure went forward.

I remember talking through the procedure, although I was very sleepy. I felt the wire going into my body through an artery in my left groin. It was somewhat uncomfortable, but not painful. It's like being at the dentist after they've numbed you and you feel the pressure of the drill in your mouth but

Thanking the audience with Lynnette and Eden at the
Living for Eden Benefit Concert for our family.

no pain. Doctor Gray checked my heart's pressures, the stent he had put in six months ago, and coiled off a large collateral artery.

I awoke in the recovery room surrounded by other children in their beds, plenty of nurses, and a lot of movement. To be honest, I felt extremely uncomfortable, and I had a lot of anxiety. I'm not sure if I had a bad reaction to a drug or what. I was discouraged and mentally drained. I felt like the character Andy in *The Shawshank Redemption,* trying to escape through the narrow tunnel he had spent years digging to freedom.

Lynnette put my socks on my feet and I put on my shirt.

Eventually the anxieties went away. I became calm and asked for some food. I asked my nurse for the popular root beer slushy many hospital kids have grown to love. I downed a few of those, got a dose of antibiotics through my IV, which they then removed, and by 10:30 P.M. we were able to pack up and head home. I still have a large bandage over my left groin that I'll take off in a few hours.

In the midst of suffering, I try to remind myself that it does end. It might seem like a million years away, but the pain ends. Some suffering lasts our whole life, but it still ends. I am comforted by my faith and knowing there is a loving God who does not find joy in our suffering but finds joy in what it makes us become.

APRIL 17, 2009

Lynnette's Thoughts on the Benefit Concert

Lynnette posted her thoughts about the Living for Eden Benefit for our family on her private blog. I asked her if I could share with you what she posted. Here is what she had to say.

"Where on earth do I start? There are no adequate words to describe this experience for us, nor are there words to express our gratitude to all of those who participated, donated, helped with, and attended this event in our behalf. It was one of those once-in-a-lifetime experiences that we have been so fortunate to have.

"Oh, how we wish everyone could have felt what we felt that night! It was an outpouring of love that was so incredibly overwhelming, and it lifted us beyond our imaginations. The concert was amazing and so much fun.

"We truly respect all of the artists who participated. They live up to the utmost definition of goodness. I wish we could thank each and every person individually who helped make this event a success on April 6.

"We know so many of you put forth a lot of effort in advertising, getting donations, etc. The funds raised will ease the financial burden we are facing with Paul unable to work and the medical expenses that will continue to come, but truthfully, I feel like the most amazing gift from this experience is the love we felt from all of you. And that is worth more than anything money could buy! We are so humbled.

"The true highlight of the evening was seeing the faces of so many beloved friends who were in attendance. We felt of your spirits and we will draw from this experience for many months to come, especially in those challenging times. Since the concert there have been many tears of gratitude in the quiet moments of our home as donations continue to silently come and as we replay this event in our minds. Thank you, thank you, thank you!

"All of Paul's siblings are wonderful, and I admire them all. They were so great as they rallied around to pull this event off. His sister, Carol Burgoyne, was responsible for the silent auction, and her organizational skills are amazing. Several of my siblings and other family members helped out too.

"Everyone that participated made this event an overwhelming success. Family and friends are life's greatest blessing!"

Lynnette Cardall

Chapter 14

"PIANIST'S COMPETITORS RALLY FOR FELLOW ARTIST"

BY CARRIE A. MOORE

DESERET NEWS

Saturday, April 11, 2009

When earnestness trumps envy and competition gives way to cooperation, great things can happen among friends, though adults—especially those in the public eye—seem often to act otherwise.

So when Russ Dixon, leader of a local band called "Colors" called a fellow musician last month to perform free of charge at a benefit concert for pianist Paul Cardall—whom some fellow LDS musicians may consider to be "the competition"—the answer "left me with goose bumps," Dixon said.

"I'd pay money myself to come and do that show," came the reply.

When at least two dozen local musicians, producers, sound and lighting technicians, and cameramen came together this week at Cottonwood High School, they added their silent "amens" to the reply Dixon heard. Each left without a dime in their pockets, though the concert was a sellout.

"Living for Eden," as the show was dubbed, was a full-blown community effort to raise money for their friend and fellow musician, whose damaged heart won't beat much longer. Cardall and his family—including his three-year-old daughter, Eden—are waiting for a phone call that says a donor heart is waiting to be transplanted into his chest. It's his last shot at being able to see his daughter grow up. After living for more than three decades with congenital heart disease, he's undergone [numberless] operations and [six] open-heart surgeries.

While Cardall's spirit is strong, his heart grows weaker by the day.

Peter Breinholt explained the connections between fellow artists in a backstage interview before his own performance.

"I got a call a month ago from Jeremy Baron," Cardall's friend and former business partner who got the benefit ball rolling. "He told me Paul was in trouble. But what Jeremy didn't realize was that behind the scenes, production people got wind of it and it started rolling. Graphic designers, artists, and all of them started calling. We had to turn people away from helping out with this. There were lots of other performers that would love to have been here."

It was a decade ago, when Breinholt had established himself and Cardall was an up-and-coming wannabe, that they first met. "He started asking if he could drive with us to shows. We went to Rexburg to perform and Paul came along. He didn't play, he just wanted to learn the music trade. After a four-hour drive up and back, we were friends."

Ryan Shupe and the Rubber Band, another local group, was on the same trip. It was the initial meeting for all of them.

"Fast forward seven years, and Paul is the guy who has a recording label, who's signing people, who has Billboard-charting albums. He's an expert with Web sites and online distribution. We've all asked for help from him in those areas. The people who he had once tagged along with are now asking him for advice."

Sam Payne, another local artist who served as master of ceremonies for the concert, said Cardall was instrumental in helping him develop his latest album.

"We never have perceived each other as the competition. Our acquaintance is around the kitchen table. We share plans and music. I think we feel a lot of love for one another and the other's music, and that makes it a pleasure to be together."

While Payne and his fellow musicians could try to grow their reputations outside Utah, "making music in this community with these people far outstrips the bottom line, at least for me." Though most would question the size of the local music market, "somehow enough grows here to fill everyone's pockets, so we can play as friends and not as competitors. That's one of my great blessings as a musician."

Kurt Bestor, the self-proclaimed "old man" of the group, said he was happy to see and be part of a unique melting pot of local artists who can come together as collaborators rather than competitors.

"I think you go through periods in your career

where you don't trust anyone and you're jealous of everyone else's gigs," he said. "But you get to a point where you feel pretty confident in your own ability, and you start thinking, 'I can learn something from this guy or that guy.' It seems good not to have to worry about jealousy."

Cardall met Bestor a few years back at a local restaurant, and the relationship began as a mentoring one. "But we quickly left that behind and became friends. He helped me with my Web site and we've done some business stuff together. . . . The guy is so humble, sweet and loving, he just makes me feel like a schmuck."

Maybe more than most, Bestor understands how serious medical challenges can turn lives upside down. Both his children were born with spina bifida.

"Without community, you don't get through this stuff. . . . I've experienced enough on the other side that I'll be forever saying yes," when a friend is in that kind of trouble, he said.

Shupe said he's watched the local "brotherhood of musicians" develop over time, and wasn't surprised by the way they all came together to support Cardall. "We love Paul. . . . I've never known anyone who has something like he has. We wanted to help out as much as we could."

Jeremy Baron was Cardall's business partner for two years and knew last summer of his friend's listing for a heart transplant. As manager for several LDS musicians and a concert producer, he put the concert together as a way to help his friend financially, whatever the eventual medical outcome is.

"We all knew going in that we can't do anything to

prolong his life. That's in the Lord's hands. We wanted to make the process as easy for him and his family as we could. None of us know how long Paul will be here. If he's going to stick around for a while, we don't want him to have a huge financial burden," Baron said.

"If not, we want things to be as easy for Lynnette, and especially for Eden, as possible. I can only imagine how difficult that would be for them."

Carol Burgoyne, Cardall's sister, was deeply involved in organizing the ticketing and silent auction aspects of the concert. Family and friends provided items for auction, as did people who heard about the effort and looked for a way to help.

"To me those were some of the neatest donations. They weren't sought out, they just saw a need and had something they offered," she said. One Eagle Mountain resident offered $200 in product from his dot-com business, and an artist who had a prize-winning painting depicting two small children donated her work.

"Everything was bid on and everything sold," she said. Some 30 volunteers worked with ticket distribution and silent auction sales, while two groups of students from Jordan and Olympus high schools served as ushers.

Several "heart moms" whose own children are suffering from congenital heart disease were there in force, Burgoyne said.

Her brother "has had such an impact on their lives because he's reached out to them, mostly through Internet correspondence. He knows what they're going through. It's just neat to see him doing that, and they've found hope in him, and reached right back to him that night."

Audience members did their part, showing up an hour before the show began and spilling onto the sidewalk outside. Local vendors provided financial support and donated several items for a silent auction.

The family of Gracie Gledhill, an infant who was one of Cardall's fellow patients at Primary Children's Medical Center, was honored with a tribute to their daughter, who died last month after surviving only a year with a congenital heart defect. Her funeral had been Cardall's only public performance since he was listed for a transplant last August.

After two and a half hours of music, the audience rose to a standing ovation as Cardall, his wife, Lynnette, and their daughter were invited on stage.

With a portable oxygen tank at his side, the man whose music had brought them all together was momentarily speechless.

"I can barely talk," he said, breathless not only from emotion, but from the walk up the stairs to the stage. "I just want to thank every one of you for supporting us," he said, arm in arm with his wife, as Eden danced happily in the spotlight.

He spoke of his fellow patients at Primary Children's, most of them decades younger than he and wondering what the future holds. "I have great faith in the future," he said. "Whether or not it turns out the way some of us want it to, I know there is a great thing called 'families are forever.'"

With that, he sat down and played the only song he's written in the past several months, dedicating the performance of "Gracie's Theme" to Dr. John Hawkins, "who is also fighting for his life." When it was finished, the little girl danced over the oxygen cord and into the arms of the man at the piano—the one who works every day at living for Eden.[1]

LIVING FOR EDEN

PART 8

Remembering a Girl Named Stephanie

There is not a week that goes by that I don't remember a little girl named Stephanie who had a profound effect on my attitude and my outlook on life.

At age fourteen, I lay in the pediatric intensive care unit after surgeons reconstructed my heart's anatomy, sleeping mostly, as my body recovered. One day, I awoke and saw, standing next to the side of my bed, a young girl who appeared to be five or six years old. She had dark hair and big beautiful eyes, and she was obviously mesmerized at my situation. I must have had a hundred tubes running in and out of me, and I still had a large one down my throat, which was uncomfortable. But here was this young girl who was very pale with a trachea tube in her neck. She could not speak, and, sadly, she appeared to be dying. Yet this little girl had

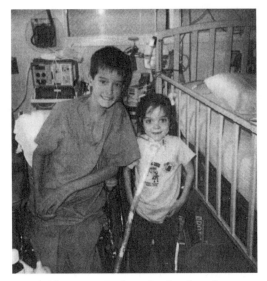

Sitting with fellow patient Stephanie Ruggles who took interest in my recovery from heart surgery. She passed away a few months later.

a smile that stretched from one ear to the other as if to say, "Cheer up . . . It'll be okay!"

Over the next few days, we became friends. I learned that the little girl's name was Stephanie. She would stop by to visit me in the PICU and eventually in my room on 4 West. She drew me a picture of her in green scrubs standing tall in a bed of colorful flowers by a tree with the sun shining down. I would show her my BYU football posters of Shawn Knight and Jason Buck, along with an autographed picture of Bruce Hurst, who pitched for the Boston Red Sox. He had graciously stopped by to see several patients the previous year while I was having heart surgery to remove the staph infection endocarditis. (His pitching helped the Red Sox defeat the New York Mets in the 1986 World Series.)

Eventually, I recovered and went home. A year later my family ran into Stephanie's mother Patsy at a grocery store, where she told us that her daughter passed away shortly after we left the hospital. She had had a form of cystic fibrosis, which slowly took her home to God. Patsy told us Stephanie loved coming down a floor to see patients, but it wore her out and eventually she died.

Many years later, as I was preparing to leave my home for a two-year mission for my church, this experience replayed over and over in my mind. I spent three weeks in a training center under a very strict schedule. We were up at 6:30 every morning, attended twelve hours of class, and hit the sack at 10:30 P.M. This began to wear on my health, and I was frustrated and became depressed. I thought about asking to be sent home. I didn't want to be a burden.

Then my mind reflected back to my challenges in the hospital, and I thought of Stephanie. For the first time, I realized the depth of her sacrifice in visiting me. She died giving of herself to others. She probably could have lasted a little longer, but instead she got out and went to the aid of others. Whether that was her intention or not, she did it anyway. Her visits and radiating smile comforted me in the hospital, and I was no longer depressed.

In that missionary training center, after being depressed

and throwing a pity party for myself, I decided to cheer up, and I repeated Stephanie's words: "It'll be okay." My mission became one of the most important experiences of my life, where I learned many of life's valuable lessons.

There is not a week that goes by that I don't think about Stephanie.

THURSDAY, APRIL 30, 2009
The Irony in Life

Life is full of ironies. A prominent thoracic surgeon who was scheduled to do my procedure, and who has saved hundreds of kids' lives, has cancer and will be unable to return to the operating room. Our thoughts and prayers are with him and his family during this incredibly difficult time.

Another one of life's ironies is that my thoughts and prayers are constantly with a family whose husband, son, father, mother, wife, or daughter will be my donor. If I only knew who they were, could I warn them? Could we stop whatever calamity is coming? This is a very sobering predicament. Like the young single mother who gives her child away to a married couple for adoption, there is an almost indescribable sacrifice that takes place.

My wife works with babies fresh from heaven, while I have a friend who used to bury people for his profession until he sold his business. On and on it goes, and the irony of life and death is fascinating, sobering, difficult, and mysterious.

This art represents the Jesus I know. "Security" by David Bowman.

Where do we find comfort in all of this? It's almost impossible for me to discuss such strange diversions in life without acknowledging my faith in a loving Heavenly Father who knows and understands all things.

A leader of my church and a spiritual hero of mine, the late Neal A. Maxwell, wrote, "Irony is the hard crust on the bread of adversity. Irony can try both our faith and our patience. . . .

"Amid life's varied ironies, you and I may begin to wonder, Did not God notice this torturous turn of events? And if He noticed, why did He permit it? Am I not valued? . . .

"Irony may involve not only unexpected suffering but also undeserved suffering. We feel we deserved better, and yet we fared worse. We had other plans, even commendable plans.

Did they not count? A physician, laboriously trained to help the sick, now, because of his own illness, cannot do so. . . .

"In coping with irony, as in all things, we have an Exemplary Teacher in Jesus. Dramatic irony assaulted Jesus' divinity almost constantly. . . .

"At the end, meek and lowly Jesus partook of the most bitter cup without becoming the least bitter. . . . The Most Innocent suffered the most. Yet the King of Kings did not break, even when some of His subjects did unto Him 'as they listed.' . . . Christ's capacity to endure such irony was truly remarkable.

"You and I are so much more brittle . . . we forget that, by their very nature, tests are unfair."[1]

One of my favorite scriptures reads, "I know that [God] loveth his children; nevertheless, I do not know the meaning of all things" (Book of Mormon, 1 Nephi 11:17). Another favorite scripture states, "The spirits of all men, as soon as they are departed from this mortal body, yea, the spirits of all men, whether they be good or evil, are taken home to that God who gave them life . . . those who are righteous are received into a state of happiness, which is called paradise, a state of rest, a state of peace, where they shall rest from all their troubles and from all care, and sorrow" (Book of Mormon, Alma 40:11–12).

Joseph Smith, a spiritual hero of mine, wrote, "I am like a huge, rough stone rolling down from a high mountain; . . . knocking off a corner here and a corner there. Thus I will become a smooth and polished shaft in the quiver of the Almighty."[2]

All of my challenges and mountains to climb have brought me closer to my family and to God. I would not trade them for all the money in the world. These things are difficult and discouraging at times, but there is much greater suffering in the world than my own. And through it all I am comforted, knowing that God is my friend.

SATURDAY, MAY 9, 2009
A Chapter of My Life

Life is full of chapters. We close one and start a new one. I am in the middle of "the heart transplant" chapter of my life, and the plot thickens as I continue to wait. It has been nine months. That's full term and my water hasn't broken! Albert Einstein said, "In the middle of difficulty lies opportunity."[3] We try to make the most of our circumstances, reflecting upon what we have learned or hope to learn from our situation. I am learning more than I could ever dream of, and I hope to pull through to share that with many more people.

The current president of The Church of Jesus Christ of Latter-day Saints, Thomas S. Monson, shared this powerful insight to happiness, "This is our one and only chance at mortal life—here and now. The longer we live, the greater is our realization that it is brief. Opportunities come, and then they are gone. I believe that among the greatest lessons we are to

Receiving the Distinguished Alumni Award at the 2009
Salt Lake Community College commencement ceremonies.

learn in this short sojourn upon the earth are lessons that help us distinguish between what is important and what is not. I plead with you not to let those most important things pass you by as you plan for that illusive and nonexistent future when you will have time to do all that you want to do. Instead, find joy in the journey—now."[4]

I continue to find comfort in my knowledge that God is good! God is close! God is my friend. He has wrapped His loving arms around my family through the love, service, and support of those who also love Him. It's a miracle.

Yesterday I was fortunate to attend the closing chapter for a few college students as they graduated from Salt Lake Community College, where I received my associate's degree. I was invited to attend by President Cynthia Bioteau and the SLCC Alumni Association. The school honored me with the Distinguished Alumni Award, which was quite shocking because it is awarded to those who've made a contribution to our community, and yet it's our community that for the past nine months has been making a contribution to my family. Matt Bunker, alumni advisor, made it clear that this award was decided upon before they knew I was sick. So I am thankful for the alumni's kindness in acknowledging my music career, which has been a tool for me to share something peaceful, positive, and uplifting in a world full of pain and suffering.

I am grateful for the Salt Lake Community College chapter in my life. Before graduating from high school, I was recruited by the Freshman Leadership Council despite my average grades, and I was offered a full-ride scholarship. I got involved in student government, where I sat on the college activities board, served as student Fine Arts chairperson and later as the student public relations vice president, and aggressively recruited new students. It gave me many opportunities to learn things that I have applied to my business and life. College was an enjoyable chapter of my life, and I had moments of nostalgia sitting before the graduates. Congratulations to all of you who graduated!

Celebrate Motherhood

On this special day when we celebrate motherhood, I want to express my love and appreciation to my wife, Lynnette, the mother of my gorgeous child, Eden. Lynnette chose a life with me knowing I might not grow old and that she might be alone for a season. Lynnette, I love you! Let's do it all over again.

I also want to express my love to my own mother, Margaret, who selflessly cared for me and my seven siblings. She was there by my hospital bedside every day and has continued to lift me up with great hope.

Where do I get my optimism? From my mother and her mother, my angel Grandma Layton, who also raised an army of good people who lift the world and make life a better experience for others.

I miss my Grandma Joy, my father's mother, whose life was extraordinary and who raised my father to be a great man with solid faith.

My mother-in-law, Ardith, passed away of cancer when my wife was eight years old, leaving behind ten children and a humble schoolteacher husband, Joel. Ardith's cancer started when Lynnette was only three (the age of our daughter, Eden). I look forward to the day when Ardith and I become great friends. Sons-in-law should always be in touch with their wife's mother.

Abraham Lincoln spoke perfectly what I feel: "All that I am and ever hope to be I owe to my angel mother."[5]

Chapter 16

PIONEER FAITH

Many of us are descendants of pilgrims, pioneers, and immigrants who journeyed from their native lands to America in search of religious freedom and a new life. Many generations later, thanks to our ancestors' sacrifice, integrity, and hard work, we enjoy prosperity, comfort, and, most important, freedom.

Award-winning author and historian Stephen Ambrose said something I'll never forget: "The past is a source of knowledge, and the future is a source of hope. Love of the past implies faith in the future."[1]

In order to truly understand who we are, we must learn about our ancestors. I recall meeting a spiritual leader in my community who knew my maternal grandparents, Alan and Mona Snelgrove Layton. He shook my hand tightly and said with a smile, "You're of good stock. Pioneer stock!" While I didn't know much about my heritage at the time, I was filled with a sense of pride at his words.

Over the years, I've learned from family conversations, research, old journals, and just plain experience, that we have a tremendous amount of strength and determination running deep in our family roots, particularly among the women.

On May 5, 1819, in Sussex, England, my great-grandmother, Mary Joy, was born. On June 20, 1843, at the age of twenty-three, she married twenty-four-year-old Edward Snelgrove in Southampton, Hampshire, England.

As they began to establish their new life together, Mary Joy and Edward heard of a new Christian doctrine being preached by missionaries from America who called themselves Mormons. The English people were being encouraged to join the cause of the restored gospel of Jesus Christ and gather to America with the Saints.

In a book published by the LDS Church Educational System, we read:

"[Mormon] elders gained audiences in private houses that had been licensed for preaching and on street corners. Aware of the poverty and illiteracy of most of their listeners, the missionaries spoke on the level of their audience, acted as common men, wore no distinguishing garb, and did not teach for hire. They quickly extended the hand of fellowship and brotherhoods, making all the people feel equal before God. The obvious sincerity of the missionaries was a dramatic contrast to the lordly attitude of the English clerics of the day."[2]

In a spirit of excitement and trepidation, the young Snelgrove couple accepted baptism and joined the new

American faith. They had little money, so they sold most of their possessions in order to fund their passage to America. In a show of support, Mary's grandfather commented, "If I were young again, I would go to America."[3]

According to a family journal passed down through the generations, Mary said, "I embraced the gospel with an honest heart and we are leaving our home and kindred for the sake of salvation."[4]

With their son Edward Jr., Mary Joy and Edward Snelgrove made the 188-mile journey to Liverpool harbor. There the young family joined 470 converts aboard the square-rigged ship *The Ellen Maria,* eighty-three feet in length, twenty feet wide at midship, and thirteen feet deep in hold at midship. She was carvel-built, rigged with a slanting bowsprit, and weighed 189 tons. This ship was one of eight sailing vessels that carried Mormon converts to the American continent.

From Liverpool, like many other organized bodies of immigrants, this group of Christian believers embarked on a journey that would change the face of America.

Legendary author Charles Dickens, who was asked to visit one of the many ships with large groups of British leaving for America, observed the many Mormon converts. In *The Uncommercial Traveller,* a compilation of news articles he wrote, Dickens said of Mormons like Mary Joy and Edward Snelgrove: "They came from various parts of England in small parties that had never seen one another before; yet, they had not been a couple of hours on board, when they established their own police, made their own regulations, and set their own watches at all the hatchways. Before nine o' clock the ship was as orderly and as quiet as a man-of-war."[5]

Charles Dickens was impressed with the Saints' sense of direction, ability to organize, and attitude of hopefulness. He said, "In their degree these people were the pick and flower of England."[6]

After several weeks of poor wind and storms, *The Ellen Maria* sailed on February 1, 1851, enjoying pleasant weather and fair winds. On March 14, the ship docked on the Mississippi River, off New Orleans, making the passage from Cardigan Bay in seven weeks.

During the journey, eight children and two adults died from fever, measles, consumption, and inflammation of the chest. Every child and many adults on board the ship suffered the measles and whooping cough.

With all of the suffering on board came also days of happiness and celebration. Six marriages and a birth took place.

The remarkable story behind this journey was the extraordinary ability of Mormon leaders to organize the people. After leaving the port, without settling in, the assigned leader over the religious expedition was President James W. Cummings, who divided the company of 470 converts into 12 divisions or wards, allotting 10 berths to each division, and appointed a president over each. Then these twelve divisions were divided into two, and a president was appointed to preside over each six, so that there were twelve companies in the steerage with a president over each, and two to preside over the whole. The second cabin was organized the same way.

In addition to the physical leadership and organization, the Mormon leaders also organized the group of people to receive spiritual strength. "The Priesthood were also organized, and presidents [were] appointed over them to see that they attended to their duties. This complete organization was found to be of great utility in preserving peace, good order, and the health and comfort of the people while on board. President Cummings and his two counselors watched over their flock with the utmost care, and in meeting in council with the brethren who had charge of the smaller divisions, they could easily learn the condition of every Saint on board. If any were sick, or in want, or in transgression, they were made acquainted with it, and they immediately adopted measures to relieve the wants of the needy and to prevent iniquity from creeping into their midst. Men were appointed to visit every family twice a day and to administer to the sick."[7] Although the Snelgroves were happy to arrive in America, illness set them back. Both Mary and her son were ill, and Edward suffered horribly from cholera. Edward Jr., almost seven years old, was sent to get medicine from the druggist. Mary thought he looked well enough to run the errand. Upon his return with the medicine for his father, Mary watched in agony as her only child dropped dead at her feet. The doctor couldn't explain the illness or why the child died.

In those days, poor and dying folks were so numerous

My pioneer ancestors from England, Edward and Mary Joy Snelgrove,
journeyed nearly 3,000 miles to settle in Salt Lake City, Utah.

that death had become a successful business. Those burying
the dead would walk down the street with a cart and cry out,
"Bring out your dead." Thus, young seven-year-old Edward
Jr. was carried away by strangers and buried in an unknown
grave. By this time, it was too late for the Snelgroves to journey with the company with which they started in England.
They had to travel alone to St. Louis, Missouri.

In order to make the journey, Edward and Mary sold
most of their remaining possessions. When they arrived in
St. Louis, they camped and waited until the following spring
to head west across the plains.

Fortunately, in Missouri the Snelgroves became friends
with a recently converted family, the Golightlys. They

discovered that Mary was pregnant, and Edward found work so they could earn the money to travel west.

When spring came, the Golightlys and Snelgroves pooled together their resources to make the long, hard journey across the plains with a large company of other Mormon converts. To their dismay, just as they were about to leave, Edward had a horrible reoccurrence of the dreaded cholera.

With confidence, determination, and faith in the God who had led them to this new religion, Mary Joy was not about to let anything get in their way again. She took things into her own hands. She said, "We are going!" People had already left for Utah and she knew if she waited for Edward to recover they would be stranded for another year. With great faith only a strong woman can possess she repeated, "We are going!"

Mary Joy traveled up the Mississippi River to Council Bluffs in Pottawattamie County, Iowa, to purchase supplies and make arrangements for the trip west. Meanwhile, the Golightlys took Edward and their wagons to Council Bluffs, where they met Mary Joy.

Council Bluffs had become the gathering point for the Saints, since the majority of Latter-day Saints had been forced out of the United States after an organized mob called the Carthage Grays murdered founder Joseph Smith and his brother Hyrum in Carthage, Illinois.

As part of the John Tidwell Pioneer Company—a group of 340 people with 61 wagons—the Snelgroves and their friends began their journey west from Kanesville, Iowa, in June 1852. The couple stayed behind a few days until Mary gave birth to their new son. They named him Edwin Stenhouse after the missionary in England who had taught them the restored gospel of Jesus Christ. The next day, the family began their long-awaited three-month journey to Utah.

Mary lay in the wagon with her new baby boy cradled in her arms. She had experienced four miscarriages in England, and she had lost her only living child fifteen months earlier. However, on the plains of America, in a new world with a bright future, she enjoyed her new son, and anticipated reaching Zion with the Mormon people, led by their prophet, apostle, and leader, Brigham Young.

Mary Joy, a healthy Edward, and little Edwin finally reached the Salt Lake Valley in September 1852. The Snelgroves were greeted by several families, who invited them to gather produce from their gardens—corn, potatoes, and whatever they needed to get by—until they were in a position to help themselves and eventually help an arriving family.

Soon the Snelgroves began to prosper. Manna began to fall from heaven as they committed their lives to God and their community. In an elegant description, Mary and Edward's daughter Mary Louisa wrote of her memories of living in the home her parents built two years after arriving in Utah:

"The piece of land where our home stood was surrounded by a 5-foot picket fence. There were neat graveled walks that came around the house and down to the front gate that opened onto the sidewalk.

"In the back yard was an orchard of fruit trees and berry bushes—currants, gooseberries, raspberries, and such. Father planted trees, shrubs, and flowers to gladden the eyes and beautify the surroundings. As small as I was, I held the young trees for Edward, my father, while he planted them.

"The front yard was laid out with flowerbeds, and flowers lined the walks."[8]

The hope, faith, determination, and sacrifice of Edward and Mary Snelgrove are representative of my pioneer heritage. Within me, I carry these pioneers' faith, their commitment to God and community, their legacy, and their hope in a bright future. I will do all I can to honor their lives.

Chapter 17

LIVING FOR EDEN

PART 9

Acts of Kindness

Acts of kindness continue to pour down upon us like a much needed rainstorm. A large group of our neighbors and members of our church congregation thoroughly spring-cleaned our yard, removing all dead leaves and weeds, pruning trees and branches, edging, mowing, straightening our mailbox with new concrete, prepping an area for a garden, putting a trampoline together for Eden, planting flowers, and much more.

What can we say? We're overwhelmed. There are kind people in the world. Amid all of the sensational headlines of war, death, and destruction, there is goodness. Generally, people have good hearts and use them. I also hope for a good heart to use it for good.

I believe there is hope for anyone in great need of help.

People can't take away your grief. They can't solve all your problems. They can't abolish your fears. What they can do, if you'll let them into your lives, is ease your burden.

Neal A. Maxwell wrote, "To withdraw into our private sanctuaries not only deprives others of our love, our talents and our service, but it also deprives us of chances to serve, to love, and to be loved."[1] He also said, "Of a truth, those who can easily bend their knees in prayer do not feel they are stooping when they bend to help a neighbor in need."[2]

Most great service and acts of kindness go unknown and unrewarded, except for that inner conscience that gently soothes the soul with comforting words saying inward, "Job well done!"

We've always tried to surround ourselves with goodness in our home and in our friends, and we try to do all within our power to lift others. I wish I had the energy to tutor relationships with every person I meet that I might find out what it is I can do to help them, lift their load, ease their pain. It's hard to be among people and not shake their hands. I miss it. I miss serving and sharing things in common and enjoying conversation. And I hope that with a new heart I might continue to share my love for life, not only through my music, but also through common friendship and private acts of kindness.

What Pulls Me Through

I've begun more iron infusions through my PICC line, which should give me a boost.

It's been a tough week. My body is tired. And I'll admit that I've been depressed at times and full of anxiety. Yet how can I feel empty? I have every reason to live and love.

What pulls me through? Others. Family. Friends. All of you. My wife is beautiful in every way. Eden is adorable.

My former bishop, with whom I served as his executive secretary in our church of volunteers, had his hip replaced. His recovery has been quick because he's a remarkable human being. He walked almost a mile to visit me using two forearm crutches. He's a man I admire and hope to one day be like.

Also our neighbor, who has cancer throughout her body, dropped off several dark red geraniums to add to the beauty of our yard. This neighbor and her husband have greenhouses, and they spend time growing all kinds of vegetation. They also have a son who has had a heart transplant. She is a remarkable woman, who, despite her illness, sits near us in church each week to thank God for what we have and hope for.

Another neighbor—a good man, father, and husband who almost died a month ago and who has been on the liver transplant list—got a call for a liver. The surgery was a success and he is on the mend. It's a miracle, and we thank God.

When I am discouraged, a tool that lifts me is music. With its varying emotions and influence, particular music pulls me through. What would the world be like without it? Pretty depressing. This past week I've been absorbing the lyrics from popular Christian artists MercyMe, in their song "I Would Die for You." It's as though they are singing my thoughts.

Finally, I had a great time Thursday watching the *American Idol* finale. I'll admit it. From a professional standpoint, you can't go wrong with young, newly discovered talent performing with icons Lionel Richie, KISS, Queen, Cindy Lauper, and others. The song that former *Idol* winner David Cook performed for his brother, who died May 2 from a cancerous brain tumor, was inspiring.

JUNE 6, 2009
The Waiting Psychosis

My wife and I have a phrase called "the waiting psychosis," which is a state of peril, a social standstill, or a lack of progression where nothing seems to be moving forward until a concluding event. This could happen to a person in my situation, who has waited a long time for life-or-death surgery, or a woman on bed rest during a difficult pregnancy, where the outcome is uncertain. It could happen to someone diagnosed with cancer, someone living in a troubled marriage not knowing if it will last, or someone losing a child to drugs,

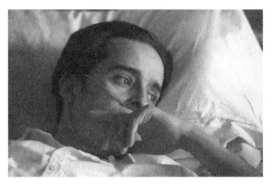

*In the quiet of my hospital room, I found myself staring
out the window and praying for strength.*

immorality, or something else. In any of these situations,
human emotion intensifies and life can seem confusing.

I can't speak for others, but I have learned some important principles in suffering. Of course, I don't have a doctor-
ate in philosophy or psychiatry, but I have experienced a great
deal of suffering. I realize many of you have gone through
far greater trials than my own. Survivors of the Holocaust
could teach us all a great deal about pain. Please permit me
to share with you a few things I've observed.

I've learned that how a person reacts to suffering affects
more than just that person. When you throw a pebble in a
pond, there is a ripple effect. How you act or react to your
situation affects those around you. It's okay to be angry, im-
patient, and frustrated. It's all right to voice your concerns to
those closest to you and talk through the problem. But how
often do we remember to tell the people in our lives how

much we love them? Do we share with them how much we appreciate their help and sacrifice in serving us? Our tough times aren't a party for them either, but together, as Martin Luther King Jr. said, "We shall overcome!"[3]

I have learned that four specific principles can help us during a difficult situation: humility, patience, courage, and service.

First, humility. Suffering will humble you, so if you aren't humble, hold on to your hat, because something at some point in your life will happen to remind you that you are powerless to change your own situation. I'm inspired by Mahatma Gandhi, a humble man, who oversaw a peaceful revolution that led India to independence and inspired movements for civil rights and freedom across the world.

Second, patience. Waiting for a desired outcome can teach you patience. Leo Tolstoy wrote, "Patience is waiting. Not passively waiting. That is laziness. But to keep going when the going is hard and slow—that is patience. The two most powerful warriors are patience and time."[4]

Third, courage. Courage can be defined as strength in the face of fear, pain, or grief. There are many great examples of people who overcame their fears and took courage as their course of action. My maternal grandfather was a captain of a gun artillery unit in France during World War II. He led men into battle, and he was wounded at least once. He reminds me of all those who face war—the darkest hour of human suffering.

Stephen Ambrose's popular book and HBO series, *Band*

of Brothers, follows the men of East Company from D-Day through the war. A few days after D-Day, they were walking down a road toward a French village when a German machine gun opened fire on them. In spite of their training, the men ducked for cover and froze. The company commander, Dick Winters, knew if his men stayed there, they would be cut down. Lieutenant Winders reacted. He stood up in the middle of the road, away from cover, with bullets whistling all around him, and ordered his men to move out. His men stared at him, not believing what they were seeing—but only for an instant. The courage of their commanding officer inspired them. They moved out.[5]

You don't have to go to war to face courage. My father-in-law raised ten children after his wife passed away from cancer. He was a schoolteacher and retired early to raise his children, who are great people.

My sister's husband chose to follow his convictions and serve a mission for his church even though his own father discouraged him from going. People like that are my heroes. They do something extraordinary even though it's hard. As C. S. Lewis said, "Courage is not simply one of the virtues, but the form of every virtue at the testing point."[6]

Fourth, service. Service is love. It is the humble act of giving of your time, talents, and whatever else you have, to help another person. Accepting service takes humility. When I realized the growth we experience in serving others, I finally understood that to deny someone else the opportunity to serve is to be selfish. David O. McKay declared, "Happiness is the end, really, of our existence. That happiness comes most effectively through service to our fellow men." He also said, "It is a *principle* the application of which promises to supplant *discouragement* and *gloom* with *hope* and *gladness*; to fill life with *contentment* and *peace* everlasting. This being true its acceptance would indeed be a boon today to this distracted, depression-ridden world. Why, then, do men and nations ignore a thing so precious?"[7] The great American poet Maya Angelou said, "My great hope is to laugh as much as I cry; to get my work done and try to love somebody and have the courage to accept the love in return."[8]

Humility, patience, courage, and service are principles we must work at. It takes time to develop them, and none of us is ever perfect at any one of them. When my chest is opened for the sixth time in my life, it won't be my doctor's first time working on a heart. He has been trained. It takes courage, humility, patience, and service to do his job. Surgery is like playing the piano. You work on your skills and spend a lot of time developing your talent. When it comes time to perform, you hope you've practiced enough to be the most effective at the most critical time. Likewise, I will hold to these four invaluable principles, which should empower me through the drama of recovery and any other future events that will challenge me. I am not perfect, and this is why I needed an imperfect heart.

Finally, I find great comfort in a statement made by one of my spiritual guides, who passed away from cancer. Neal A. Maxwell declared, "We tend to think only in terms of our endurance, but it is God's patient long-suffering which provides us with our chances to improve, affording us urgently needed developmental space or time."[9] I pondered that word, *long-suffering,* a word used to describe God by great spiritual leaders in nearly every Christian denomination. What does the word mean? To be long-suffering is to be stoic, charitable, understanding, and forgiving amid difficulties. I've learned that if we endure our challenges with humility and patience—and ponder all that we've endured, no matter what the circumstance—we will be stoic through the storms of life that our family, friends, or associates face. We will be even more endowed with power to reach our hand down and grab their hands to pull them up.

Chapter 18

"SON OF KSL EDITORIAL DIRECTOR DIES AFTER BEING TASED BY POLICE"

BY JOHN HOLLENHORST

KSL NEWS REPORTING

Tuesday, June 9, 2009

WASHINGTON COUNTY—A 32-year-old man died Tuesday afternoon after he was tased by a Hurricane police officer.

Brian Cardall is the son of KSL's Editorial Director Duane Cardall.

He and his wife, who is six months pregnant, were traveling south on State Road 59 just outside of Hurricane after visiting his family in Salt Lake City.

According to his wife, Cardall, who has a recent history of mental illness, was having an episode that prompted them to pull over to medicate.

Once stopped, Cardall got out of the vehicle and began to run down the road.

His wife called 911. Not long after, she found out he had been tased and was unresponsive.

CPR was administered on scene. Cardall was taken to the Dixie Regional Medical Center where he was pronounced dead.

The Washington County Sheriff's Office is investigating.

In a press release on its website, the Sheriff's office writes: Police and medical personnel responded to a call for assistance with an agitated subject on State Route 59 this afternoon in Washington County. During the incident, a Hurricane City Police Officer deployed a taser and the subject lost consciousness. The subject was treated within moments by EMS personnel, but was pronounced dead after being transported to the hospital.

Cardall was a doctoral candidate in biology at Northern Arizona University.

In a statement his family said, "Brian is a wonderful son, brother, father, and husband who loved being with people. He was full of personality and wanted to make a difference in this world. He was working on his PhD in Molecular Ecology at Northern Arizona University. He loved being in the outdoors and with his daughter Ava and beautiful wife Anna. We will miss Brian but are comforted by our faith."[1]

Chapter 19

LIVING FOR EDEN

PART 10

TUESDAY, JUNE 9, 2009

Tragic News Concerning My Brother, Brian Layton Cardall

I have struggled my whole life with a severe heart defect, while Brian experienced some mental illness. Rarely did Brian have the kind of episodes that triggered this horrific tragedy. The public should know that Brian was a wonderful son, loyal brother, loving father, and faithful husband who loved being with people.

Brian was a great friend. He brought so much joy to our family and had the biggest heart in the world. He was a good man striving to learn how to be a better man. It was an honor to know him in this life and call him brother. Our family will miss Brian but we are comforted by our faith in a loving

My brother Brian Layton Cardall dancing with
his daughter, Ava Skye, a few days before his death.

Heavenly Father whose grace is sufficient enough. Here is to our brother Brian. God speed, my friend. You are free to exercise the spiritual depths of your heart. We love you!

Chapter 20

"I KNEW YOU WOULD COME"

*E*ven though I was just five years old, I still remember the cold December day in 1976 when my new baby brother Brian and my mom came home from the hospital. There was little snow on the ground that day as my siblings and I walked home from school. We walked through the front door of the house and saw Mom holding our little brother. My father filmed just about every event in our lives, and there he was with the old 8-millimeter camera. My younger brother David and I each chewed on a piece of taffy as we looked at the camera and proudly said to our Dad, "Look, it's our new brother."

Once Brian was old enough to move from a crib into his own bed, the three of us shared a room together, while our three older sisters had a room down the hall. Like a scene from *The Brady Bunch,* we all shared the same bathroom, but we were fortunate to have two sinks and a large tub. Mom could wash three of us at once.

During the summer, we spent a lot of hours digging in the sandpile in the backyard after family dinner. When the sun began to fall, Dad squirted us down with the hose before we jumped into the tub to clean up for bed. David and I enjoyed digging in the dirt because we thought we actually might reach China, while our younger, more curious brother Brian, who was fascinated with the outside world, looked at the dirt to see what he could find. He observed the various rocks within the soil and the thousands of different textures of sand. Later, we came to understand that Brian appreciated God's creations in a way we could not comprehend until we matured into adults.

My sister Jane came to us in 1979, and our family was completed in 1982 with our youngest brother, Craig. As kids, we believed we always had two up on *The Brady Bunch,* and we wondered why they ever needed their housekeeper, Alice, when our father and mother were so skilled at organizing a workload for their children. Gordon B. Hinckley, who served as president of The Church of Jesus Christ of Latter-day Saints from March 12, 1995, to January 27, 2008, said that during his childhood, his family didn't have an automatic dishwasher but that it was his automatic duty to wash the dishes. My brothers and sisters and I felt the same way.

On Saturday mornings, my siblings and I would get up early to watch cartoons like *The Hall of Justice, Yogi Bear,* or, later, *The Smurfs.* We would eat a bowl of cereal my mom had poured the night before, and we would look at the job chart, which listed each of our names and our chores for that day. Dad even drew a rough-sketched map of our yard, with subdivided weeding assignments and our names written on the spot we were assigned to tackle. I don't remember Brian ever complaining, but the rest of us moaned and groaned about working on the only day we had off from school. Still, in church the following day, we always sang with pride:

> *Saturday is a special day.*
> *It's the day we get ready for Sunday:*
> *We clean the house, and we shop at the store,*
> *So we won't have to work until Monday.*
> *We brush our clothes, and we shine our shoes,*
> *And we call it our get-the-work-done day.*
> *Then we trim our nails, and we shampoo our hair,*
> *So we can be ready for Sunday![1]*

When Sunday came, my mom loaded everyone up in our white station wagon and drove us several blocks to church. Dad was usually already there because he served on our stake high council, a group of priesthood leaders with stewardship over Church members who live within a stake, or a specific geographical area. In each stake are several wards or congregations. When I was eight years old, Dad was called to serve as the bishop over our ward, which consisted of nearly one thousand people.

Mom still remembers the Sunday when we forgot all about Brian. We had loaded up in the car and made our way to the church. As we sat on the third or fourth pew, taking up

Jane, Brian, David, and Paul Cardall in a family portrait.

the entire row, Mom noticed Brian was missing. "How in the world could I forget about Brian?" she asked herself sadly. Leaving us there, Mom drove home. When she walked in the house, her heart sank as she saw Brian in his white shirt and tie, his hair combed poorly, sitting on the couch. With his big brown eyes, he looked up at her and said with a smile, "I knew you'd come."

We grew up under the guidance and care of a loving mother and father who taught us principles of virtue, love, work, and loyalty. They made good men out of their sons and great women out of their daughters. There was a sense of unity and purpose that only a loving couple could provide. We lived in the world but were not part of it, at least in a spiritual sense, yet our parents carefully prepared each of us to leave home and embark on our own journeys.

Even after all that has transpired in our lives, no matter where we are or what trouble we are in, our parents and, most important, our Heavenly Father will find us. And like my brother Brian on that Sunday afternoon he was left home alone, we can joyfully say to our parents, "I knew you'd come."

※ *Chapter 21* ※

LIVING FOR EDEN

PART 11

THURSDAY, JUNE 11, 2009

My Brother's Death

As our family copes with Brian's tragic death, two scriptures come to mind. One is from the Book of Mormon, and it reads: "I know that [God] loveth his children; nevertheless, I do not know the meaning of all things" (1 Nephi 11:17). Another scripture reads, "He that hath faith in me to be healed, and is not appointed unto death, shall be healed" (Doctrine and Covenants 42:48).

SATURDAY, JUNE 13, 2009

A Sobering Week

This has been one of the most difficult weeks in all my life. My brother dying is beyond comprehension. The tragic way in which it happened is hard to understand. I am so sad.

Brian was my friend, my dear sweet friend. He was the kindest man I know, and he always avoided contention and wanted everyone to be happy. He wouldn't hurt a soul verbally or physically. He spoke with open arms, asking for patient understanding, and he approached everyone with love and concern. He was a genius and an artist, he had a brilliant mind, and he was one of the most gifted young scientists of his generation.

I will never be the same. Yet somehow through this entire nightmare, I am at peace. God is with me. The experiences of my life continue to strengthen me and give me comfort. I have the greatest family and friends in the world. Everyone should feel this much love.

Adversity is a hard thing to bear, but there is hope of a brighter day and of times to reflect on the many wonderful blessings of life.

Chapter 22

FISHING WITH BRIAN

$\mathcal{A}$t an early age, my younger brother Brian developed a deep love for the outdoors and wanted to understand the natural world. The summer after he finished high school, he worked as a personal fly-fishing guide in central Utah, helping city folks learn how to fish. Instead of buying flies at an anglers' store, Brian captured flies and other insects out on the river and took them home in cups or plastic bags. Then, in his room, he would study each insect and replicate it with a hook, sewing needle, thread, colored feathers, and anything else he could find. His goal was to pattern his hand-tied flies as closely as possible after the species itself. When I used his flies on the river, I caught more fish than when I used flies purchased from a fishing store. Brian's understanding of ecology was a gift from the Creator, and the flies Brian tied were works of art.

After my brother left his job as a fly-fishing guide, he prepared to leave on a two-year mission for The Church of Jesus

Christ of Latter-day Saints. He had been called to serve in Bilbao, Spain, and I had recently returned from serving two years in San Bernardino, California. Before he left, we decided to head up one last time to one of our favorite rivers, Currant Creek, located forty-five miles southeast of Heber, Utah. With our sleeping bags, food, fishing gear, and a Chris LeDoux cassette tape, we headed east past Park City towards Highway 40, eventually pulling off the side of the highway onto a dirt road. I don't remember what we talked about during the two-hour drive, but when we arrived at the river, we set up camp and fished for a few hours in the early evening. As the sun fell and the cool night air crept in, Brian and I rolled out our sleeping bags to camp beneath the stars, which were brilliant without city lights to dim their glow. There were many patterns I had never seen before. Brian pointed out the Big Dipper, the Little Dipper and its Polaris, Gemini, North Star, Orion, and many others. As the conversation deepened, I asked my little brother, "How do you know God exists? With all that is out there in the universe, and with so many unanswered questions here on earth, and contradictions between science and religion, how do you know there's a Creator?" While staring into the heavens, Brian paused a moment and then replied, "Can't you feel it? Look up at the stars and all around you. The only thing that can explain all of this are the words to 'How Great Thou Art.'" I asked him if he knew the words by heart, and he quoted them.

O Lord my God, when I in awesome wonder
Consider all the worlds Thy Hands have made,
I see the stars, I hear the rolling thunder,
Thy power throughout the universe displayed;

Then sings my soul, my Saviour God, to Thee,
How great Thou art! How great Thou art!
Then sings my soul, my Saviour God, to Thee,
How great Thou art! How great Thou art!

When through the woods, and forest glades I wander,
And hear the birds sing sweetly in the trees,
When I look down, from lofty mountain grandeur
And hear the brook, and feel the gentle breeze.

And when I think that God, His Son not sparing,
Sent Him to die, I scarce can take it in,
That on the cross my burden gladly bearing
He bled and died to take away my sin.

When Christ shall come, with shout of acclamation,
And take me home, what joy shall fill my heart!
Then I shall bow in humble adoration
And then proclaim: "My God, how great Thou art!"[1]

(Words: Stuart K. Hine
Music: Traditional Swedish folktune/adapted by Stuart K. Hine
Words and Music © 1949 and 1953 by The Stuart Hine Trust. All
rights in the U.S.A. except print rights administered by EMI CMG.
U.S.A. print rights administered by Hope Publishing Company,
Carol Stream, IL 60188. Used by permission.)

🦝 *Chapter 23* 🦝

LIVING FOR EDEN

PART 12

TUESDAY, JUNE 16, 2009

Wonderful Tributes to My Brother

The funeral for my brother Brian was perfect—one of the most beautiful services I've ever attended. Our celebration for his extraordinary life and the love shared among family and friends transcends this world.

My siblings delivered wonderful tributes. Brian's father-in-law, David Schmidt, taught us beautiful doctrine pertaining to Jesus Christ and His resurrection.

Professor Stephen M. Shuster spoke of Brian as one of the most gifted scientists of his generation. He even said, with great humility, that Brian was *his* teacher and kindly corrected his work at times.

Finally, my father paid a wonderful tribute, and counseled us—reminded us—that we believe in the principle of

With an oxygen tank and a Milrinone drip,
I placed flowers on Brian's coffin at his graveside service.

forgiveness. Although people should be accountable for their actions, we believe in forgiveness.

I am continually in awe of my father and mother in their ability to lead and guide our large family, with twenty-two grandchildren, through this difficult time. We have forgiveness in our hearts. Through God's grace and mercy, it is a beautiful feeling.

As far as my health, I know it won't be long before a heart comes. I continue to pray with all my soul for the donor's family, who I now understand will walk our same path and share our same emotions. I am going to fight that much more to live better for them and for my brother.

I want to live and continue on what my brother would have wanted me to do.

Chapter 24

A TRIBUTE TO BRIAN

*H*ere is the message delivered at Brian's funeral by one of his colleagues, Stephen M. Shuster, Professor of Invertebrate Zoology, Department of Biological Sciences, of Northern Arizona University.

A Trained Scientist

He had a bachelor's degree from Utah State University. There he became interested in newts and garter snakes and had the chance to work with one of the great professors of herpetology, Dr. Edmund Brodie Jr.

Brian went on to publish this work as an undergraduate student. The fraction of all undergraduate students who ever finish college is less than 50 percent. The fraction of such students that ever engage in scientific research is less than a tenth of this number. And the fraction of that number of students who actually complete their research and publish it in a scientific journal is less than a tenth of that number.

At a very early age and stage in his career, Brian Layton Cardall showed he had the ability to make important contributions to science. But as an undergraduate, Brian hadn't tired of discovery yet.

Brian went on to complete a master's degree at Utah State University in Dr. Karen Mock's laboratory. There Brian showed, using skills he was developing in molecular genetics, that certain native fish in Lake Bonneville, Utah, were actually two distinct species. Okay, two different species instead of one. Why should this be so important?

In fact, this is one of the most fundamental contributions any biologist can make. It is a biologist's job to give humanity a better understanding of how the natural world works. Brian showed us all something we had never known before; that is, until Brian decided to consider this aspect of nature himself.

Brian gave the scientific world a way to see things differently than they had seen it before. He was excited about using his skills as a biologist and a scientist. He had shown he could make important discoveries, and again, he had published his work. But as a master's student, Brian hadn't tired of discovery yet.

Brian contacted me about becoming a graduate student in my laboratory. I was familiar with some of Brian's work, and the chance to have a seasoned scientist join my lab as a doctoral student seemed almost too good to be true.

Brian and I discussed several options for graduate support and decided he should apply for a Science Foundation Arizona fellowship, a recently established organization designed to invest early in individuals who have the highest potential to drive innovation and scientific research in Arizona. Brian seemed a sure bet to receive this funding, and indeed he was awarded a fellowship. But as a Science Foundation Arizona Fellow, Brian hadn't tired of discovery quite yet.

Brian decided to shift his interests yet again to investigate what is now known as "community genetics," the study of how genetic variation within one species may influence the distribution, abundance, and reproduction of other species. This new discipline links molecular and evolutionary genetics to population, community, and ecosystem processes. Community genetics has fundamental implications for conservation biology. And this was a connection that I believe Brian, who was passionate about conservation, could simply not resist.

Brian's work took several different avenues. His cottonwood work focused on locations in Arizona and Utah, in which an invasive plant known as salt cedar or tamarisk, had changed riverbanks that had once been populated by cottonwood trees. Brian's work has already shown that there may be particular genetic variants of cottonwoods that are resistant to invasion by salt cedar, a discovery that could revolutionize river restoration efforts in areas where salt cedar is abundant. But as a community geneticist, Brian hadn't tired of discovery quite yet.

Brian became interested in Diorabda beetles, another invasive species that happens to like to eat tamarisk. And consistent with community genetics theory, Brian showed that beetles preferred to eat certain salt cedar plants and avoid others. Brian had begun work, independently, with scientists at the University of California–Santa Barbara to understand the genetic basis of such preferences. But again, as a conservation biologist, Brian hadn't tired of discovery quite yet.

Brian's interest in animals was never too deep below his cheerful exterior because Brian had almost single-handedly developed molecular genetic

Dr. Edmund Brodie Jr., Utah State University professor of herpetology, congratulating my brother Brian on receiving his master's degree.

markers that he and I planned to use to explore sexual selection in marine isopods in Mexico.

Brian had also grasped statistical methods I was exploring to understand how animals such as beavers can change ecological communities by preferring some cottonwood trees and not others. Brian had grasped this approach so thoroughly that he was already correcting my work and gently and patiently showing me places where my calculations were in error. But, you guessed it, as a theoretician, Brian hadn't tired of discovery yet.

Brian immersed himself in each of these fields, and by the spring of 2009, he had comfortably assumed his place among the intellectual cream of young Arizona scientists.

At Northern Arizona University, he had become the standard against which all Science Foundation Arizona Fellows were judged. He was a leader among the graduate students in our department, and he had the respect, admiration, and affection of all of the members of my laboratory.

Brian loved his work. It never seemed to represent work to him. He seemed charmed by the beauty and complexity of nature, and Brian was wearing the largest of his infectiously large smiles when in the field with his daughter Ava, she riding on his shoulders or strapped to his chest, facing outward so she could see the world through her father's inquisitive and perceptive eyes.

Brian Cardall was one of the most outstanding people I have ever known. He was a consistently friendly, hard-working, intelligent, witty, and even-tempered guy. He was a kind and gentle human being. He was a devoted father and a caring husband. And Brian had all of the intellectual, creative, and scientific tools he needed to become one of the most outstanding scientists of his generation.

His work spanned questions and applications from molecules to ecosystems. But Brian, although he is no longer with us, does not seem to be tired of discovery quite yet.

Brian's work and love of nature lives on in his publications, those that have already explained so much about the natural world, as well as those on cottonwoods and tamarisk, on tamarisk and beetles, and on marine isopod crustaceans, all of which are very close to completion and eventual publication.

It is a tragic understatement to say that Brian Layton Cardall will be missed. But I believe Brian's discoveries and insights have a long and bright future ahead. Brian's publications will do much to keep us all from growing tired of discovery. I have been and continue to be inspired by Brian Cardall: my student, my colleague, and my friend.[1]

LIVING FOR EDEN

PART 13

FRIDAY, JUNE 19, 2009

What Would Brian Do?

Between my brother Brian and me in age is my brother David, who lives in Las Vegas with his family and works as a construction manager. He builds things, and he is good at it. After Brian's funeral, David had to get home early for some business meetings in Los Angeles. On their drive home, David and his family stopped at the place where Brian tragically slipped into the next world. They left some flowers and said a prayer, thanking God for Brian's life.

After arriving home, David went to L.A. for his meetings. He was on his way to the airport when he realized he still had two hours before his flight was scheduled to take off. He asked himself, What would Brian do if he had this time? David said, "That's right. I'm going to the beach." He loosened his tie, kicked off his shoes, and got his feet wet. He sat on the shore and observed one of God's beautiful creations. David found a metaphor in the waves. As they would crash into the shore, some waves crashed hard, while others were softer. He thought of waves as trials and challenges that continually crash upon us. They don't stop; they just keep coming. They may calm for a while, but they return. And every now and then there's a tsunami.

I'm grateful for what David did in asking himself, What would Brian do? Amid storms and trials, we should observe the wonderful world in which we live and thank God every day for the beauty that surrounds us. Find peace in a sunset. Look for it in the color of the flowers and grass. Go fishing. Climb a mountain. Loosen your tie, kick your shoes off, and get your feet wet.

Yesterday, when I met with my transplant clinic, I learned that the call could come any day now. I am climbing that list, and after what my family has been through I will fight like crazy to live. Bring it on! And one year from now, June 9, 2010, the anniversary of my brother's death, with a new heart—my own rebirth—I will climb Mount Olympus, a peak in the majestic Wasatch Range, in honor of my brother. He was a beautiful man.

Brian died before we could donate his organs. But Intermountain Donor Services (IDS) was able to retrieve some bones and tissue to transplant and help someone out there. I am grateful for this. Our family was given a beautiful certificate with the ironic logo "Donate Life."

For more information on organ donation visit: www
.donatelife.net/

How Is It That I Get By?

People have asked me over and over how it is that I get by,
even now, with the tragic death of my brother who I am so
close to. How do any of us get by? For me, it's almost impossible to explain a spiritual feeling deep in my soul that keeps
me focused and reminds me that life is temporary, but that
how we choose to act in this life is eternal. It doesn't make
life easy, but the hard times are a bit more tolerable.

The lyrics of "Bring the Rain" by MercyMe feel like my
life's anthem.

> *I can count a million times*
> *People asking me how I*
> *Can praise You with all that*
> *I've gone through*
> *The question just amazes me*
> *Can circumstances possibly*
> *Change who I forever am in You*
> *Maybe since my life was changed*
> *Long before these rainy days*
> *It's never really ever crossed my mind*
> *To turn my back on you, oh Lord*
> *My only shelter from the storm*

But instead I draw closer through these times
So I pray

Bring me joy, bring me peace
Bring the chance to be free
Bring me anything that brings You glory
And I know there'll be days
When this life brings me pain
But if that's what it takes to praise You
Jesus, bring the rain

I am Yours regardless of
The dark clouds that may loom above
Because You are much greater than my pain
You who made a way for me
By suffering Your destiny
So tell me what's a little rain?[1]

Learn more about my faith and the root of what helps me in times of trial at http://thedoctrineofchrist.blogspot.com/

TUESDAY, JUNE 23, 2009
A Powerful Poem

I heard a great poem by Rudyard Kipling, author of *The Jungle Book*. Kipling's son, John, was lost in action during the Battle of Loos, in September 1915. His body was not recovered until long after his father's death and the war's end. These words reminded me of Brian.

"Have you news of my boy Jack?"
Not this tide.
"When d'you think that he'll come back?"
Not with this wind blowing, and this tide.

"Has any one else had word of him?"
Not this tide.
For what is sunk will hardly swim,
Not with this wind blowing, and this tide.

"Oh, dear, what comfort can I find?"
None this tide,
Nor any tide,
Except he did not shame his kind—
Not even with that wind blowing, and that tide.

Then hold your head up all the more,
This tide,
And every tide;
Because he was the son you bore,
And gave to that wind blowing and that tide![2]

This poem was published to accompany some articles written about the Battle of Jutland in May 1916—the largest naval engagement between British and German warships during the war. British losses—of men and ships—were heavier than that of the Germans, although the German High Fleet never attempted to come out of port again for the rest of the war.

WEDNESDAY JUNE 24, 2009
Begin Living Today

With all that's gone on these past two weeks, I have not discussed my involvement with the Primary Children Medical Center's Miracle Network Telethon. The hospital was able to raise more than 2 million dollars to help some of the families that need financial assistance. The outpouring of love from our Utah community is amazing. They talk about the many miracles happening daily at the hospital with the kids, but the miracle is the money raised.

In regard to my current health situation, I have some energy during the day. I continue taking a lot of medication, visiting the clinic every other week, and undergoing minor tests. It's been more than ten months (308 days) since I was listed for a heart. I know others have been waiting two years, so it's not bad. I have a routine down, and amid all of the chaos of life I have never been so happy in my marriage, as a father, and as a friend. There is a peace inside me that I know comes from all of the prayers empowering me to hang on, fight on, and conquer this wild dream!

A vital principle I've learned during this process is best expressed by a saying I once heard from a Baptist minister: "Stop waiting for life to come tomorrow, begin living today. Don't miss what's NOW because you are looking for what's NEXT!"[3] His statement is brilliant. Don't live life looking to the future for happiness. Rather, live today! Celebrate everything you have. Celebrate your family and friends. Material things are worthless. How you treat your family is priceless. Did you think to pray? Did you make someone smile? Did you say, "I love you"?

Stop waiting for life to come tomorrow. Begin living today. Don't miss what's NOW because you are looking for what's NEXT!

WEDNESDAY, JULY 1, 2009

The Highest Peak of Our Lives

Utah weather is wacky. One day it is cool with rain, and the next day dry and a hot 95 degrees. Even though I'm outside as much as I can be, I feel a peaceful storm coming in which I will get a transplant and experience a challenging recovery. I could get a phone call from my doctor at any moment saying, "Paul, we have a heart for you."

I have confidence in my surgeon's ability to pull it off. I don't doubt that. But I fear the recovery. Will I be claustrophobic? I have felt uncomfortable in the past during simple procedures. Will I go crazy or feel extremely restless? I've experienced some of those feelings before in the hospital, and this is my greatest fear. I'm not afraid of the surgery and the physical pain as much as the fear of having no control over my mind and body. I'm sure these questions and emotions are natural. Despite these insecurities, I am at peace knowing that the entire team is prepared.

I am also preparing my mind and soul. My daughter,

wife, and whole family are on my mind. And now with the sudden death of Brian, I want to fight that much more. I want to live for these people whom I love.

Brian continues to inspire me. He climbed the face of mountains and accomplished many great things. As my wife and I prepare to climb one of the most incredible peaks of our lives, I'm ready and comforted because I know he'll be close by. Others won't see, feel, or notice him, but I know he'll be there along with so many others pulling me up that steep mountain of recovery.

In the meantime, Lynnette, Eden, and I have been spending more time together as a family doing a few fun things. I have some renewed energy, which I attribute to everyone's prayers and good medicine. In fact, last night we went for ice cream at Baskin Robbins. Eden always orders the clown, bites off all the decorations, and then offers to trade desserts with my wife. She will eat most of Lynnette's ice cream and then want to swap back, leaving her mother an empty cone. We laugh. Eden is a character.

My sweet girl has been asking about Brian. We went to the cemetery and she wanted to see what she calls the "pretend" Brian. We told her that he's not there and has gone to be with Jesus. Trying to explain death to a toddler is quite difficult. Ironically, the day before Brian's death, Eden and I were walking outside and saw a dead robin. I said, "Look, it's not moving."

She asked, "Why not?"

"Because he died," I answered. "The life inside of him

went to be with Jesus, leaving his body behind." I got a shovel and we dug a little hole in a section of our garden. I put the bird in the ground and we covered him with earth.

Eden said, "I want to see it again." I told her we couldn't, at least not now, but possibly someday.

I didn't realize the profound impact of all of this dying talk until a couple evenings later. It was after Brian's funeral, while Lynnette was working, and Eden was curled up next to me. With some sadness and frustration on her face she said, "Dad, I don't want you to go with Jesus." I told her I would do my best but if I had to go be with Jesus, Brian and the bird would take good care of me. I think she understood.

WEDNESDAY, JULY 8, 2009

Our Rocking Chairs

Please forgive me for not responding to all of your considerate comments, kind expressions, and wonderful messages. I have read each one with great appreciation and sincere humility.

The past month has been a bittersweet experience. My brother's death knocked the wind right out of me. Because of that, I've chosen to focus more intently on my family and their needs. I love and admire every one of you. Thank you for your friendship.

Due to our situation, I said to my wife, "Go out and buy our rocking chairs. I don't want to wait to grow old with you. I would love to sit with you on the porch today!"

*The rocking chairs I encouraged Lynnette to buy so we wouldn't
have to grow old to sit on our porch together.*

Lynnette brought home two beautiful chairs. The only problem is that we need a third chair for Eden. My sweet little girl is jealous and wants her own chair. She cracks me up! So tomorrow we'll start looking for a third chair. The store evidently sold us the last two black rocking chairs. I'm sure we can find a pink one for our little diva.

SATURDAY, JULY 18, 2009

My State of Mind

Eden asked me the other day if I was Blumpoe the Grumpoe, referring to one of her bedtime stories. My roller coaster of emotions is challenging to deal with at home when it's just the three of us. I do my best to control my frustrations, to try not to impose my own suffering upon others. I count my blessings. But when my three-year-old notices a problem, it breaks my heart.

The truth is I'm tired. It's been a tough month! Having poor health, waiting for a heart transplant, experiencing Brian's disturbing death, watching my daughter grow up too quickly before my eyes and the burden my caring wife is undertaking sobers my soul. In addition, I know folks suffering in their own sets of circumstances. I ache to get well and give back to everyone who has selflessly cared for my family and me, as well as reach out to those who need help.

It is in the quiet hours of my personal darkness that I continue to call out to God, our Heavenly Father, to help sustain me. He has never failed me. I have only failed Him because of my own inadequacies and weakness. Amid my circumstantial frustrations, I look to the future with hope. I see the sun rising from the east, bringing new life and a sense of purpose. I'm excited and determined to fight. Give me freedom! Give me life! Yesterday, I was reading Michele Gledhill's heartfelt blog for her deceased little angel, Gracie. I was inspired and uplifted by a quote she put there by my spiritual leader, Thomas S. Monson: "Mortality is a period of testing, a time to prove ourselves worthy to return to the presence of our Heavenly Father. In order to be tested, we must sometimes face challenges and difficulties. At times there appears to be no light at the tunnel's end—no dawn to break the night's darkness.

Brian holding his daughter, Ava.

We feel surrounded by the pain of broken hearts, the disappointment of shattered dreams, and the despair of vanished hopes. We join in uttering the biblical plea 'Is there no balm in Gilead?' (Jeremiah 8:22). We are inclined to view our own personal misfortunes through the distorted prism of pessimism. We feel abandoned, heartbroken, alone. If you find yourself in such a situation, I plead with you to turn to our Heavenly Father in faith. He will lift you and guide you. He will not always take your afflictions from you, but He will comfort and lead you with love through whatever storm you face."[4]

In addition, as I continue to contemplate the life of my brother Brian, I have found great joy and satisfaction in the precious opportunity of reading his journal. His soul and his words inspire me, and I see life through a new lens. At an early age, while working as a missionary in Spain, he began compiling a journal full of his thoughts. It contains a list of nearly one hundred goals and quotes that became personal mottoes. He wrote he didn't want "a day-by-day summary of the routine they call life, but a record of the highlights . . . It could be that I die tomorrow, and these pages [journal] go left blank. Or it could be that I live to be a hundred and slip into my eternal rest with a treasure of satisfied ambitions. That isn't for me to decide. But it is for me to decide how I use the precious time that I have been granted. I've always believed that life is not just meant to spend time existing, but to spend it living. Dreams are the very sustenance of life. And as dreams are achieved, life's purpose is achieved, and life is truly lived."

I have chosen to follow the counsel of Thomas S. Monson and my brother Brian. Therein, I am confident any one of us can find peace, strength, and hope for a better tomorrow beginning by living today. In fact, here a few inspiring quotes Brian wrote in his journal that I am also adopting as my personal mottoes.

"Yesterday is but a dream, tomorrow but a vision. But today well lived makes every yesterday a dream of happiness and every tomorrow a vision of hope."—Sanskrit proverb[5]

"Happiness is a state of activity."—Aristotle[6]

"The best and most beautiful things in this world cannot be seen or even touched. They must be felt within the heart."—Helen Keller[7]

Enjoying time away from the hospital with my beautiful wife.

"Experience is not what happens to a man; it is what a man does with what happens to him."—Aldous Huxley[8]

"God left the world unfinished . . . the pictures unpainted and the music unsung and the problems unsolved, that man might know the joys and glories of creation."—Thomas S. Monson[9]

"Simplify. Simplify."—Henry David Thoreau[10]

As I climb my own mountain, I know there will be many helping me carefully ascend to the top, renewed with life.

THURSDAY, JULY 30, 2009
I Love My Wife

Today, I want to express my love for my family, my friends, my sweet daughter, Eden, and most importantly, my wife, Lynnette. What I have learned of romantic love and the beauty of marriage I have learned from her. When I speak of hope for a bright future, she is the sun rising from the darkness, bringing warmth that moves through me. We have a pure love that no one can take from us. It's a bond, a friendship that defies this world. Our love is bound by our commitment to each other. I pray daily I may live worthy of her love and give her the respect she deserves, no matter what comes our way.

According to Jeffrey R. Holland, "The first element of divine love—pure love . . . is its kindness, its selfless quality, its lack of ego and vanity and consuming self-centeredness. 'Charity suffereth long, and is kind, [charity] envieth not, and is not puffed up, seeketh not her own' (Moroni 7:45)."[11] My wife has all of these qualities.

Again, thanks for all your thoughts, prayers, faith, fasting, or however you choose to worship, on our behalf. God is my friend, and though life is a wild ride and difficult at times, it is also incredibly satisfying. I would do it all over again!

The Gledhill family (Callie, Tom, Taylor, Michele holding Gracie, and Max).

SATURDAY, AUGUST 1, 2009

Gracie's Theme

When I was born with a congenital heart defect in 1973, my parents almost lost me. Today, according to the American Heart Association, heart defects account for about 30 percent of all birth-defect-related deaths. No one should have to lose a child, yet these hard things happen daily.

Many years ago, I was fortunate to travel with Richard Paul Evans, who wrote the *New York Times* best-selling book *The Christmas Box,* inspired by parents who've lost children. He had invited me to compose an album of piano music inspired by his work. As we toured the country together, I met thousands of parents who've experienced the death of a child. It's a cross so hard and difficult to bear that I'm not sure I can truly understand the depth or pain. Needless to say, I am inspired by those who've crossed that difficult road and climbed that impossible mountain. They are some of the most kind, compassionate, humble, and open people I know.

Tom and Michele Gledhill are two such parents. They dealt with congenital heart disease even before Gracie Jean was born on March 20, 2008. Their journey of ups and downs in fighting to keep their daughter alive is a powerful example of love, hope, and faith. And although Gracie passed away on March 2, 2009, after a difficult heart transplant, the Gledhills know she has returned to a loving God.

Gracie's brief mortal life empowers her family and those who knew her with virtues of humility, strength, compassion, openness, understanding, and a love for others. Their daughter was an angel, a gift, sent by God to bless lives.

What do I take away from knowing families like the Gledhills? Never give up! Never quit! Never lose sight of having faith in God. And in the end, if any of us are called home to the God who gave us life, before what some may call our time, we can declare, "I have fought a good fight, I have finished my course, I have kept the faith" (2 Timothy 4:7).

SUNDAY, AUGUST 9, 2009

Did You Just Say "Esophagogastroduodenoscopy"?

If my toddler read this entry, she would probably ask if I learned it watching *Sid the Science Kid.* Unfortunately, when

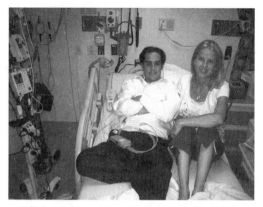

The hospital room became my home away from home.

it comes to medicine, I learn from experience. The twice-daily Lovenox shots I shied away from almost eight months ago are now as painless as brushing my teeth. Designers of the needles just need to make Lovenox needles a little sharper to get through building scar tissue. And so it goes with lab work, tests, and now minor outpatient surgery.

Cardiologists Melanie Everitt and Angela Yetman have been concerned about possible esophageal varices, which are extremely dilated sub-mucosal veins in my lower esophagus. They are most often a consequence of portal-vein hypertension, commonly due to cirrhosis of the liver. Patients with esophageal varices have a strong tendency to develop bleeding. It would make an already difficult transplant recovery much more challenging.

And so this past Monday, I underwent a minor outpatient

procedure called an upper GI, where a doctor uses a scope or tube to directly examine the upper gastrointestinal tract. The procedure was performed by Dr. Dan Jackson at Primary Children's Medical Center in Salt Lake City. An anesthesiologist put me to sleep. Dr. Jackson found no major concerns. There are a few bad veins in the lower third of my esophagus, but nothing worth banding.

While I was under anesthesia, Dr. Everitt was kind enough to arrange the removal of my existing PICC line and the insertion, in the same vein, of a double-lumen PICC, so that I can begin receiving nutritional formulas containing salts, glucose, amino acids, lipids, and added vitamins this coming week. It is called total parenteral nutrition (TPN) and will help my body stay tuned up for major surgery.

My father and my wife volunteered to keep me company while I waited for and came out of my procedure. We've been through this before, so they came equipped with laptops and books to keep themselves occupied. I often feel sorry for the many parents who've come for the first time with nothing to do but pace the floor and watch *Hannah Montana* on the children's hospital network television. Of course, I'm not sure what's worse—having surgery, or watching Zack and Cody on the Disney Channel and learning how "suite" their life is!

*My sister-in-law Anna helping Ava leave a handprint
in her father's temporary gravestone.*

TUESDAY, AUGUST 11, 2009

Family Reunion

Our family enjoyed a reunion in Park City, Utah. As expected, the gathering was not the same without the presence of Brian. His wife Anna and spirited daughter Ava joined us, and we mobbed them with love.

With all that has transpired in our lives, our Cardall family was still able to gather in humility, love, and friendship. We also had a lot of laughter.

After the reunion, our family went to the Salt Lake City

Cemetery to set a temporary headstone on Brian's grave. I say temporary because the city suggests letting the ground settle before a permanent tombstone is set.

My younger brother David and my dad built a concrete base. As the concrete settled, Anna helped Ava make hand and foot prints in the concrete and write the words "I love you, Daddy."

I wish people had what I've been fortunate to enjoy. Along with the overwhelming love I feel from Lynnette and Eden, my parents are still together and they love each other. L. Tom Perry declared, "In a world of turmoil and uncertainty, it is more important than ever to make our families the center of our lives and the top of our priorities."[12]

THURSDAY, AUGUST 13, 2009

Day Two in the Hospital

Yesterday I had to be admitted to Primary Children's Medical Center's PICU. I am now receiving an intravenous nutrient supplement as well as an increased dose of Milrinone, which helps the heart muscles function. This is all in an effort to tune my body up and make me strong for the transplant. Dr. Everitt also submitted a request to get me 1-A status on the waiting list for a heart. I believe there are three other people in Utah who are 1-A. When the heart comes is all according to the will of the Lord. I have always been in His hands.

The staff is friendly and I've enjoyed spending some brief

time with Dad, Mom, and Lynnette. I look forward to seeing Eden today. She went to her preschool orientation with Lynnette and will enter school next week. I'm proud of her progress. Eden is a remarkable human being. She is spirited, strong, beautiful, intelligent, and polite, and she tries to be kind to others. I love and adore her. Lynnette continues to amaze me in her ability to guide Eden. Together, they make a wonderful team and have a tender friendship.

Day Four in the Hospital

We received bad news this morning. My protein-losing enteropathy is worsening. In addition, the final results of my upper GI exam are back, and there are concerns with bleeding in my lower intestine. The hard truth is that it makes transplant surgery more difficult because doctors were already concerned with bleeding during the procedure. Now they have another challenging issue to deal with. Once more, doctors are not giving me good odds. In fact, I appreciated Dr. Everitt saying my life is "entirely in the Lord's hands."

I had a tender moment with Lynnette over the phone. Lynnette shared with me her powerful faith in God. She knows without question that the Lord is in charge. I am in His hands. She is open to His will, even if that means that I die. This is the most comforting expression I have received from my eternal friend and companion. She also experienced a significant dream where we were standing in the hospital hallway and the surgeon said, "I knew many times going into surgery that the child would not survive. But I chose to operate anyway because you have to put your faith in God that He'll come through for us."

I plan to go ahead with the transplant. I want to fight to live. I accept and know that God has all power to heal me. My life is entirely in His hands. It always has been. And I pray I may be worthy of His love, which no person can escape. Jesus is the Christ. I believe that Joseph Smith restored these truths in the nineteenth century. Our family is bound by the sealing power of love, which is eternal. As I am in God's hands, so are my wife and my daughter.

MONDAY, AUGUST 17, 2009
Day Six in the Hospital

My Dad and Mom came up to the hospital yesterday with my brother Craig and his wife Heather. They had been fasting all day, according to the traditions of our faith, which means they had not eaten or drunk anything. The intent was to strengthen their faith so as to add more spiritual power so my brother and father could pronounce a special prayer. Once more, my father and brother reiterated the many miracles of my life. Dad gave a beautiful blessing, which brought a powerful Spirit in the room. Since then I have been extremely comforted. All is well! The Lord is present, and I only pray

I may live worthy of His kindness to me. I pray daily for a comforting feeling to permeate Lynnette's soul and that Eden might continue to enjoy each day without sadness. I have full faith in God's ability to heal me through the hands and minds of my skilled medical team. I am submissive to His will.

I e-mailed my family to thank them. Here is a copy of that e-mail:

> Thank you for all of your love! We feel it so strongly . . . And with all that is transpiring, we'll need your faith and prayers even more. This morning, my doctors revealed that they are very concerned about a few new critical issues with bleeding in my bowels during my transplant operation, which may or may not be controllable. They're scratching their heads as to what to do. My cardiologist said I am in the hands of the Lord. On Monday my medical team will rally to come up with a miracle. We probably will still go ahead with doing the transplant: Please pray for my medical team (Dr. Everitt, Dr. Yetman, and Dr. Kaza).
>
> Ultimately, that is how my life has been—one miracle after another. The Lord has been extremely generous, and I thank Him daily for this experience. I am surrounded by all of you whom I love deeply. We are all in the loving hands of our Heavenly Father. No matter where we run or try to hide, we cannot escape His love. It will find us. It will bring us back to His arms. His love will heal us.

I cannot sit still. For someone to suggest my life might almost be over, I choose to fight and continue doing what I would do each waking day, which is to shout from the rooftops that God is our Heavenly Father. Jesus has the power to heal us from our own pain and suffering. He takes our burdens from us. He is doing that now for me. That is how I can smile and face this with dignity.

If you get a moment, please take time to watch some of the videos on my faith blog, http://thedoctrine ofchrist.blogspot.com. I hope you'll share its message with others who need help amid adversity.

Also, in thinking of Brian and all that has transpired this past year, I found comfort this morning in re-reading a powerful address Neal A. Maxwell gave at BYU in 1974. It is titled "But for a Small Moment."[13] Here is the link: http://speeches.byu .edu/reader/reader.php?id=6066.

One-Year Blog Entry

As an adult, I am beginning to know the meaning of the Apostle Paul's words to the Romans, "We glory in tribulations . . . knowing that tribulation worketh patience; and patience, experience; and experience, hope" (Romans 5:3–4). It is true. I have been blessed my whole life to have severe congenital heart disease. I am far from perfect, so I needed this in my life to teach me things I could have never learned without it. As a result, I am a witness of God's hand in our lives. I've observed many miracles in my own.

Last Wednesday, I was admitted to the pediatric intensive care unit to begin receiving additional Milrinone and nutrients intravenously. I'm also beginning some physical therapy. These changes are an effort to help my organs hold steady so my body is prepared for the challenging transplant. In addition, I am getting some much-needed rest. . . .

The bleeding in my bowels is serious because with the transplant surgery, the blood must be thinned with Heparin for a lengthy time so I don't throw a clot and have a major stroke. Because of scar tissue from previous surgeries, the risk of bleeding in my chest area is already a great concern. My chest will most likely remain open and accessible for a week. In addition, now my bowels may be permanently damaged. The hard truth is I may bleed to death.

I have always believed that Someone greater than all of us runs the show. I've witnessed too many miraculous events to believe otherwise. I've also felt such comforting and peaceful emotions during hard times, which are inexplicable in words. I can't deny feelings.

I was with my friend, author Richard Paul Evans, on one of his book tours when I heard him say to an audience of Christian believers: "If we look at life like a ball game, God is not an umpire who sits and looks for failure. He's more like the father in the stands cheering us on."[14]

Philosopher and spiritual leader Neal A. Maxwell wrote,

"God loves us and, loving us, has placed us here to cope with challenges which he will place before us. I'm not sure we can always understand the implications of his love, because his love will call us at times to do things we may wonder about, and we may be confronted with circumstances we would rather not face. I believe with all my heart that because God loves us there are some particularized challenges that he will deliver to each of us. He will customize the curriculum for each of us in order to teach us the things we most need to know. He will set before us in life what we need, not always what we like. And this will require us to accept with all our hearts—particularly your generation—the truth that there is divine design in each of our lives and that you have rendezvous to keep, individually and collectively."[15]

God has been extremely generous, kind, and loving to me. I am surrounded by such love and support through from family, friends, and strangers, whom I see as brothers and sisters. I ache for others without such love to feel that same strength and power. Doctors have the skills to heal the body. Friends heal the mind.

My God and your God has provided me with a wonderful medical team whom He can inspire. They are schooled and prepared to work miracles. And through them, I know God can perform many wonderful things according to His will and the faith of those who believe in Him.

And so at this time, I humbly ask each of you to please pray for my gifted and skilled medical team of doctors, surgeons, nurses, technicians, and more at Primary Children's Medical Center.

As Kenneth Cope sings in one of my favorite songs, "I Will Not Be Still":

I am a witness of His miracles and His mercy.
I put my future in his hands, knowing he's made me all I am.
I put my faith in him and truth begins to speak.
His power is real and it moves me until I will not be still.[16]

SUNDAY, AUGUST 23, 2009
Sacred Piano

With all that's transpired this past year, I've put aside my music career to focus on family and getting a new heart. I have been able to maintain contact with fans by way of newsletters, and I have consulted with a few musicians. Nonetheless, it's been difficult and a financial challenge as a father to put work on hold.

In the beginning, I canceled over twenty gigs, not knowing if I'd be able to perform. In addition, I stepped away from the recording studio. My self-run instrumental label, Stone Angel Music, released only one record, from guitarist Ryan Tilby in the past year. And yet, musically, I couldn't be more full of emotion and appreciation. It's as though music is flowing so deeply inside of me that it will burst forth into symphonies offering praise to God for His kindness and mercy

In August 2009, my record label helped me release
Sacred Piano, *a collection of my most personal songs.*

amid suffering. He has taken good care of my little family. It's
hard to sit still and not share something.

I'm grateful to Shadow Mountain Records. They reached
out to me earlier this year in an effort to help me keep sharing my music. As a result, this past week they've released an
album called *Sacred Piano* on my behalf. It's been interesting
to sit back and let them do all of the work.

Sacred Piano came out of my desire to share fifteen of my
most personal songs from my fifteen-year career, in relation
to this sobering experience. The album features original and
arranged piano compositions. In addition, while at home I
was able to record three new pieces on my old grand piano

*With time running out, I continued receiving last-resort
IV drip medications for severe heart failure.*

for the CD, including "Gracie's Theme," "Amazing Grace,"
and "Were You There?"

This past week, I had a couple of radio interviews over
the phone from Primary Children's Medical Center. We discussed everything from how I feel about waiting for a heart
transplant to recording music.

TUESDAY, SEPTEMBER 1, 2009
Hospital Life

Hospital life has made it more difficult to come up with
something wonderful to say. The truth is I am tired and anxiously hoping to get the show on the road.

During my three weeks living in the hospital, doctors have given me intravenous nutrition. In addition, I'm getting a steady stream of Milrinone through IV.

I deeply and sincerely appreciate all of your prayers, thoughts, letters, e-mails, comments, and support. I'm overwhelmed by your love and care.

Throughout this past year, your kindness has constantly reminded me of the words in Matthew 25:35–36, 40: "For I was an hungred, and ye gave me meat: I was thirsty, and ye gave me drink: I was a stranger, and ye took me in: Naked, and ye clothed me: I was sick, and ye visited me . . . Verily I say unto you, Inasmuch as ye have done it unto one of the least of these my brethen, ye have done it unto me." I am one of the very least of these, and I am grateful for your willingness to follow Jesus.

There is more fluid in my lungs, and I'm having trouble breathing. As a result, I'm receiving more doses of Lasix, and an increase in oxygen requirements.

Since I am more tired, doctors have changed my visiting hours from 5:00 to 8:00 P.M. I deeply and sincerely appreciate your visits, as well as the privacy you are showing our family at this time as we approach the final months of our dilemma.

THURSDAY, SEPTEMBER 3, 2009

The Thick Fog of Adversity

As I sit in my hospital room looking out my window, I see smog hovering over the Salt Lake Valley like a thick plague. Each year, wildfires bring our city a cloud of smoke. Although it looks miserable, I know people are going on with their lives. Eventually the rain will come, the smog will fade, and once more the valley will be restored to its beauty.

Our lives are full of these moments when the thick fog of adversity surrounds us. Yet somehow we adapt. We plow ahead and move forward with our lives as best we can. We choose how we are going to handle such a crisis. Within each of us is the ability to transform our wounds into wisdom.

"If you're going through hell, keep going," said Winston Churchill.[17] And from the brilliant Jazz pianist Duke Ellington, "A problem is a chance for you to do your best."[18]

Most of us are in the midst of hard adversity right now. As one who is struggling each day to carry on, may I humbly assure you that God, our Heavenly Father, will send the rain so that each of us might recognize the beauty in our lives.

SATURDAY, SEPTEMBER 5, 2009

A Father's Love in a Dark Hour

As I lay awake last night in my dark hospital room, which has become my home, I remembered the many nights I would lie next to my daughter in her room as she drifted off to sleep. As a toddler she didn't like being alone at night and was afraid of having the lights off. We read books and said prayers. I would turn out the light and continue lying next to her. Slowly and peacefully she would fade off, knowing her dad was nearby.

There is a beautiful analogy with such a precious memory. In my own darkest hours, I know we have a kind and loving Father in Heaven close by, and I'm not afraid. He's there to help each of us feel peace so we might peacefully endure the dark periods.

SUNDAY, SEPTEMBER 6, 2009

Facing the Future

Last night was hard. As the sun was setting, I went outside to the patio overlooking the Salt Lake Valley to soak in the evening air and think. This hospital has become my home. I have a new family in the nurses and a few of the doctors. Yet I have a life outside of this one where I have many responsibilities, which seem impossible to attend to within these walls. I'm away from my wife, and it's challenging to understand her own suffering. It breaks my heart that she is alone and sleeping without me.

I'm continually amazed by the kindness of so many people. Acts of service are numberless and I feel overwhelmed.

One such act was a gift from artist Patricia Christensen.

Artist Patricia Christensen painted this beautiful portrait of our family.

I commented to her many months ago how much I enjoyed her artwork. Within a month, she called and said, "I'd love to paint your family." Of course, we couldn't turn down such a priceless gift.

We joined Patricia and her husband, Ladd, at Wheeler Farm in Midvale, Utah. They took several photos of our family, and over the next several months Patricia worked her magic.

The other evening, Patricia and Ladd unveiled her painting, which now hangs in my hospital room. I knew parting with such a time-consuming piece of art was difficult.

As I lay in my room staring at the painting, which captures our little family walking down a path, I've named the piece "Facing the Future."

Thank you, Patricia Christensen, for your act of kindness.

❧ *Chapter 26* ❧

LIVING FOR EDEN

PART 14

THURSDAY, SEPTEMBER 10, 2009

The Heart Is Here

POSTED BY LYNNETTE CARDALL

Hello to all our much-loved friends. This is Paul's wife, Lynnette, posting from Paul's ICU room. We are deeply grateful and thrilled to share with you that Paul has received his NEW HEART!!!!

The transplant went very well, much more smoothly than expected. He continues to make progress, and we continue with prayers in our hearts that all will go well from here.

We are overwhelmed with joy for this gift and blessing. We recognize that this incredible blessing is a result of the love and prayers of so many. Paul continues with a breathing tube but has been periodically awake to communicate by writing.

Paul wanted me to share this statement with everyone.

My family waiting in the surgical waiting room for word of a
successful surgery (left to right: My brother, Craig; my father, Duane;
Lynnette's sister, Carla; my mother, Margaret; and Lynnette).

He writes, "I am alive because of the medical team, this community, and my Savior, who healed me." Once again, thank you for all your support, love, and prayers. We will periodically update this blog as things progress.

A dear friend of ours encouraged us to hang on to a simple truth and that has pulled us through to today. That truth is that miracles happen.

All our love.

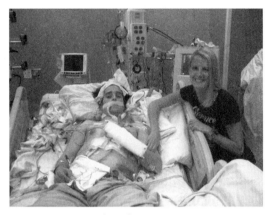

Recovering in the pediatric intensive care unit.

FRIDAY, SEPTEMBER 11, 2009

All Is Well

POSTED BY LYNNETTE

We continue to marvel at the progress Paul is making. If you can believe it, he is off the respirator and has been talking and joking like his old self between periods of rest. We are still in shock! He still has several indwelling lines, chest tubes, drains, and lots of medications, but all the equipment and bandages seem invisible when you see his great smile.

We sense from Paul a great deal of energy that is anxious to come out when his body is able to comply. The anticipation of the great things that we will see from him in the future with this newfound energy is exciting. We are all just awestruck at the steps he is making toward recovery.

Hours after my heart transplant I was visited by my first pediatric cardiologist George L. Veasy, accompanied by adult congenital cardiologist Angela T. Yetman, MD, and Edward B. Clark, MD, medical director of Primary Children's Medical Center in Salt Lake City, Utah.

What a gift from God this has been, as the miracles continue to come. And what a gift a selfless family has provided for us. We are deeply overcome with love for them and their sacrifice as we see the new heart beating in Paul's chest.

Please continue to pray for a smooth recovery, as we still have obstacles to overcome.

As we read a few of your earlier comments to Paul while he was still on the ventilator, he was so overcome with emotion that it was difficult for him. We treasure all the comments, well wishes, and prayers you continue to send our way. We are richly blessed.

Chapter 27

MY MEMORY OF THE TRANSPLANT

*A*s the second week approached in September 2009 my thoracic surgeon came into my room and discussed the surgical procedure with Lynnette and me. We were both elated to know Doctor Kaza had recently returned from his honeymoon. He looked refreshed and ready to work. Quiet and reserved, it is hard to imagine that this brilliant man is only a year older than I am.

We discussed my upcoming surgery and what would be done when the time arrived. Dr. Kaza's passion for thoracic surgery and his wisdom concerning what he and his team would do was deeply inspiring and reassuring. He drew a simple diagram on a piece of paper and explained how he would remove my football-size heart without causing me to bleed to death. Not much of it made sense, but, to my understanding, he would hook me up partially to the heart-lung machine through the femoral artery in my leg, relieving my heart of some of the work. Then after deflating a part of my heart, they would cut open my chest and do some major repair work while they waited until his team had arrived with a donor heart.

While Doctor Kaza was in my room sharing his surgical strategy he looked up at the painting by Patricia Christensen on my wall that I've entitled "Facing the Future." "That's a nice painting," said Doctor Kaza as he studied it. Then after a few more minutes of conversation he looked me in the eyes and said with deep sincerity, "Paul . . . when the time comes . . . I will work on you as though you are my own brother . . . Until that time, interact with some of these children here in this hospital. You can be very helpful."

The following Tuesday morning—on day 384 of my wait for a donor heart—I was sitting in my green overstuffed reclining chair talking with Lynnette and Dr. Yetman, who has become like my own sister, when Emily Bullock, a key member of my transplant team came into my hospital room with an expression of barely contained excitement.

Dr. Yetman joked to Emily, "With that look on your face I hope you're here to tell us good news."

After a brief pause, Emily said, "Actually . . . there might be a heart for you. We'll have a confirmation for you this afternoon." Our faces lit up in unison. I felt the same kind of excitement and emotion as I did sitting in another hospital several miles away when my wife's ob-gyn told me he was going to deliver our baby within a few hours.

Emily left the room and while Lynnette reached her

sister to bring our daughter up to the hospital, I called my parents.

"There's a heart for me," I calmly said, though my eyes were wet.

"Okay . . . Here we go . . ." said my mother on the other line.

I replied, "It won't be confirmed until later this afternoon. Either way, within twenty-four hours we may possibly know the outcome of all of this."

As I anxiously waited for my daughter and other family to arrive I had time to be alone with Lynnette to talk quietly and pray. I hoped God would extend my life. I had experienced fear, grief, happiness, and joy during those 384 days I waited for a donor heart. As I prayed and pondered life once more through an eternal lens, I felt warmth in my soul that can only come from a loving God. Over many years I had come to know Him as my friend and Father in Heaven.

In the afternoon, close to 6 P.M., the news of a donor heart was confirmed. Within twelve hours, early the next morning, I would be on an operating table looking forward to my unknown future. Waiting 384 days had given Lynnette and me time to think through everything. I'm not sure we would have been as prepared had I had the transplant earlier. By this time we were submissive and willing to do whatever God had planned for us. One thing I knew with absolute certainty was that my next state of awareness, following the deep sleep of anesthesia, would be in some form of heaven: either surrounded by familiar faces like my brother Brian, my grandparents, and other friends who've passed away, or I would awake to the divine smile on my wife's face.

That evening my parents and siblings arrived. My brother, David, and his family drove from Las Vegas, while my sister, Rebecca, made arrangements to fly in from Dallas. With almost all of my siblings and their spouses gathered in my room we had a family prayer. We thanked God for this experience and asked a blessing to be upon all those involved in the operation and, most important, upon the family who had just lost a loved one.

Saying good-bye to Eden and later Lynnette was more difficult than all of the physical ailments I had become familiar with, including all of its needles, post-anesthesia anxiety, oxygen 24/7, PICC line, and more. I remembered the false alarm of the past Christmas when I was on the operating table about to have a transplant when one of the surgeons called it off. Prior to going to the hospital that evening, nervous and unsure of my future, I went into Eden's bedroom as she lay sleeping. I stared at her in her bed. I cried. Here was this three-year-old girl peacefully sleeping, who later that Christmas Day might not have a father. I prayed while standing above her and asked God to help her when that day came. This time, as I was about to go through with the real deal, having doctors assured me it was an amazing heart and feeling optimistic, I hugged and kissed my little girl and told her I'd see her soon. I don't think she understood the depth or serious nature of what was happening. She did know I was very sick, but she had become accustomed to that since

I started carrying around an oxygen tank when she was two years old. You have to love the innocence of children because, amidst all that was happening, Eden was excited that she was going on an airplane to Texas to play with cousins for a week and that she would be able to play in their swimming pool.

Between my mother, father, siblings, and me we were well educated in saying good-bye because we had done this so many times before with previous surgeries. Only this was different. We were humbled by our grief and love for Brian. His death had been an unusual turn of events and a challenging period in our family history. His death solidified our family unit as though God put His personal stamp of approval on our lives. God extended a surge of love and strength in our family that enabled us to have a calmness and peace as once more we said good-bye prior to this dramatic surgical procedure.

Our family believed that when this was all finished, I would have a perfect four-chamber heart for the first time in my life. I would survive congenital heart disease and be able to do things I've never done before, such as thrive in the mountains without getting altitude sickness, walk up the stairs in a football stadium without looking for an elevator, dance with my daughter, bike a long distance, and hike mountains.

We are all products of our parents, and I couldn't have asked for a better situation for growing up and learning important values and principles. My parents are loyal, committed to one another, and deeply in love. My parents also had raised our family to be strong and close to God. I can't even think of a time when my parents had chosen something in their life over the needs of their children.

My family left, and I was finally alone with my wife, whom I had promised before God on our marriage day that we would be together not just until death, but also beyond. Pulling us through the dark, our source of strength was our hope and knowledge of an eternal plan designed by our kind and loving God, whom we'd grown close to through prayer and our desire to do good. If I died, though separated for a season, we knew we'd be together again.

We spent the evening talking in my hospital room, which had become my home. Nurses accommodated Lynnette with some pillows, sheets, and blankets. Eventually, because of exhaustion from the day's events, I suggested we go to sleep so we would have enough strength for the morning. That was difficult to do, but we knew we both would need our rest.

A nurse woke me up at 4 A.M. to begin preparations for surgery. My family arrived with little sleep. I had to wash with special anti-bacterial soap to prepare my body for the surgical procedure. When you enter the operation room for this challenging surgery you must enter clean. If a part of me was unclean I could get an infection and have further complications. I was touched by the symbolism of this simple act of preparation that reminds me of preparing myself to be worthy and clean to stand before God. I put on a clean hospital gown and was ready to make my journey. I fully believed I was prepared for not only the operation, but for the outcome.

Surgical techs came into my room and said, "Doctor Kaza and his team are ready for you in the OR." The time was here. Still wearing oxygen and an IV PICC line in one of my veins, I wrapped my arms around my gracious, kind, and loyal wife. We exchanged some very personal affection. I assured her we would see each other again and more than ever hoped it would be soon.

The technicians wheeled me down the hallway with my family walking beside me. We approached the entrance to the surgical unit and were greeted by one of the anesthesiologists, who was ready to get me started. Once more my family and I exchanged words and signs of affection.

The medical staff wheeled me into the surgical room, and I saw around twenty people wearing green hospital gowns, masks, and gloves. They were all busily preparing instruments, computers, and a wide variety of other essential items for the challenging surgery.

As a musician, the display of organized tools and people looked like the typical set up for a big concert with all of the stage crew, producers, musicians, lighting techs, engineers, monitors, instruments, chords, and more preparing for a big show. As I observed this magnificent display I understood the art of surgery, and a part of me wanted a tour. Finally, my anesthesiologist said, "I've got you set up and you're going to start feeling a little sleepy." I kept still on the table and continued enjoying light conversation with the team surrounding me until I drifted off.

I had no idea how long I had been asleep when I began to gain consciousness. Much like any other evening's sleep, things were a bit blurry at the first. I felt someone's soft warm hand, and I knew immediately it was Lynnette. As I focused my eyes upward on the side of my bed, there was my wife with her beautiful green eyes smiling down upon me and saying something to effect, "Everything went well." I felt very emotional. It wasn't just that I then knew the surgery had been a success, but it was because here before me was heaven on earth in the form of my wife.

Within minutes I recognized other family members in the room and a team of medical professionals working on the machines that surrounded me. Tubes of all sizes were running in and out of my body. I remember tubes in my jugular vein, one in my left arm just above the hand, several into my chest draining fluid, a catheter, a blood pressure cuff on my right arm, a saturation or oxygen monitor on my finger, a tube down my trachea for airflow, and much more. Yet I didn't pay attention to these because I was so caught up in the smiles on the faces of my family. We had just experienced a miracle orchestrated by our Heavenly Father.

Less than two days later my trachea tube was removed and I was able to speak. Up until that time I communicated by writing messages on a white board, mostly asking questions.

Over the next few days I was busy trying to regain

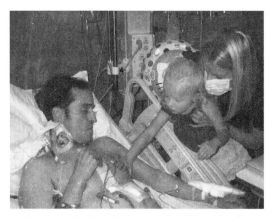

Eden feeling the beat of my new heart on her tiny hand.

strength, although I couldn't leave my hospital bed. The tubes began to come out one at a time. Each one was somewhat traumatic, but the very idea of having one after another removed gave me the strength and enthusiasm to encourage the doctors to take them out.

Finally, when I had fewer tubes and I didn't look as scary, we decided that we could bring Eden in to see her dad for the first time with a new heart. She wore her black tap shoes, a little brown skirt, and her hair was all done up like she was going to church. With her beautiful little smile and spunky personality she lit up the room. Lynnette had prepared her well for what to expect. She pointed to some tubes and asked what they were, but she mostly focused on seeing her dad. The visit ended up even being a little playful. Lynnette lifted

Eden up so she could put her hand over my chest and feel the pulsating rhythm of a powerful healthy heart.

I said, "What should we do next?"

With her childlike voice she copied my question, "What do we do next, Dad?"

I said, "When I get home."

She replied, "You get all better!" She then proceeded to do a cute little tap dance on the hard hospital floor, just as if everything were normal.

Chapter 28

"WITH A NEW HEART . . . , PAUL CARDALL BEATS ODDS YET AGAIN"

BY CARRIE MOORE

DESERET NEWS

Thursday, September 10, 2009

From tragedy to destiny in just over 90 days.

That's what family, friends and fans of LDS musician Paul Cardall were struck by Thursday morning, with word that his long-awaited heart transplant was successfully performed at Primary Children's Medical Center.

At 36, Cardall was the oldest Utah patient with [his type of] congenital heart disease to have survived to his age without a transplant. Cardiologist Angela Yetman said she's "never seen anything like" Cardall's determination to keep living and the optimism he has.

"He's come through this as if he hasn't had cardiac surgery. He's sitting up in bed talking and making jokes," she said Thursday. "I think he's benefitting from everybody's prayers and his own faith. He's got me convinced. I've known him for the last year, and I certainly can't find a better explanation."

It's a story a novelist might conjure up, but for Cardall and his family, it's another adventure in a life so surprising to medical personnel that the heart surgeon who thought Cardall would likely die as an infant made his way to the hospital for congratulations.

The donor heart was implanted by surgeons little more than three months after Cardall's brother Brian Cardall died June 9 next to a highway in southern Utah. Police had Tasered him when he was found running naked there during an episode of mental illness.

Though the Cardalls have long been grateful for the hope offered through organ donation, Brian Cardall's death put the entire family squarely into the shoes of donor families who make the decision to give organs and tissue from deceased loved ones to others. Today, they empathize in a visceral, palpable way.

Though Brian Cardall's manner of death didn't allow for organ donation, he was able to donate other tissue and bone, his father said. Noting the entire family has long prayed for those who are now experiencing their own grief so Paul Cardall could have a chance to live, his father, Duane Cardall, had a message Thursday for the donor's family, whom they will never meet. Confidentiality agreements prohibit the release of any information on the donor.

"We hope they experience the same degree of comfort that we experienced when Brian was able to become a donor," he told the *Deseret News* shortly after seeing his son in the recovery room, listening to his iPod.

It's the yin and yang of going from being a donor family to being recipients of the same kindness that prompted at least one friend who learned of the transplant to quip simply: "Miracles happen."

Paul Cardall's wife, Lynnette Cardall, said when her husband was first listed for a transplant in August 2008, "we felt a sense of guilt that someone's sorrow was going to be our joy. But I know many who have gone through this experience that were very grateful they could donate. It's one wonderful, final thing they could do for their loved one."

She said watching her husband being wheeled out of his room and into surgery was a different experience from the "false alarm" they had last Christmas Eve, when he was prepped and wheeled in for surgery, only to be told [there were problems with the heart and it could not be used].

"At the time, I wondered if I had said everything I wanted to say, and does he realize how grateful I am for him and what if I can't express that later," she said.

"There was a sense of peace this time. We all felt it was going to go fine, and I didn't have those worries. I don't know if it's because we had more time to share those feelings," she said. "He had lots of odds against him, and with how incredibly risky the surgery was, his will to live and do more with his life was stronger and overpowered those odds."

Cardall's surgeons told the *Deseret News* several months ago that his will to live was a big factor in their hope for his future.

Even so, he had grown weaker in recent weeks, which moved him up on the transplant priority list.

He has been hospitalized for the past month, and his heart—diseased at birth—had grown well beyond its normal size.

While medical personnel see that as a sign of severe illness, some would argue that the physical size of his sick heart grew as his compassion for others with congenital heart disease has become a source of hope for those who read his blog online at mytricuspidatresia .blogspot.com.

He routinely writes of children who suffer much as he did and the impact they have on those who love them. His latest song, "Gracie's Theme," was written for fellow transplant patient Gracie Gledhill, a child who died last spring shortly after receiving a new heart as he waited for a new one of his own.

Dr. George Veasy, who became "Uncle George" to Cardall during his childhood through ongoing treatment and several surgeries, showed up at Primary Children's Thursday morning to help the family celebrate.

Now in his 80s, the renowned pediatric cardiologist listened as Duane Cardall recounted their first encounter 36 years ago. Paul Cardall was a newborn in trouble, and Duane Cardall was standing outside Veasy's office door—unbeknown to him—while Veasy was engaged in a phone consultation with another surgeon.

After hearing Veasy say, "I'm afraid this kid isn't going to make it," Duane Cardall said he couldn't have imagined Thursday's reunion following the transplant. "I told him, 'Here we are 36 years later, and he's made it again!'"

In the recovery room on Thursday, "they were trying to keep him sedated, but he was very aware of what is going on," his father said. With a large breathing tube in his mouth, he couldn't speak, but he was given a whiteboard to write messages to his wife and parents.

The first one: "Tell me about the surgery." After his wife explained how smoothly things went, he pushed: "Be specific," he wrote, asking about possible complications, which she was able to assure him "weren't an issue."

He also wrote a message specifically to those who have followed his story in the *Deseret News,* as well as on his blog or in person: "I am alive because of the medical team, the support of this community and my Savior, who healed me."[1]

Chapter 29

LIVING FOR EDEN

PART 15

SATURDAY, SEPTEMBER 12, 2009

Thank You for Helping Me Achieve This Miracle!

I don't know what to say that could convey my gratitude to all of you involved in this miracle performed by our Heavenly Father through His children.

I've witnessed tender acts of prayer, hope, faith, scientific gifts, talent, surgical wisdom, and other acts of kind service to me. I am grateful and feeling good.

And yet, at the same time, I recognize the deep loss a family is feeling at this time.

Also, I have many tender feelings for the many heart babies who've left us to go back home to God. I hear their voices when I am sleeping and am grateful to know many of their names. Their history is written all over the halls of this sacred institution. I continue to pray for those who still

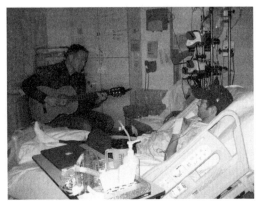

Christian artist and friend Kenneth Cope entertaining me post-transplant.

remain, who fight for a future with their families, who fight to enjoy this world.

I am still with you and will continue to pray for you and exercise my faith in your behalf.

The everlasting cycle of life's ups and downs is difficult to imagine. There is so much sadness and yet so much joy in my heart today. I am truly grateful. I feel spoiled. One of my ecclesiastical heroes said, "Each of us have sort of a rendezvous with destiny. And the world needs more kindness."[1] I feel that the Lord has been kind to me, and I have much to do to honor the goodness of those who've fought this fight with me. I pray I may be worthy of your kindness and love.

I can't doubt that this is a miracle God performed.

I attribute all these many blessing and newfound

perspective to the God of Heaven, my wonderful wife, daughter, family, friends, and numberless strangers who are my brothers and sisters, who share a common bond.

God is a tender, loving Father who is cheering from the stands, helping us improve with practice and time.

He tenderly and patiently awaits our running home into His open arms. He is soft-spoken and it takes great effort to hear His influence unless we are in such hard situations.

I love you all and look forward to doing whatever I can to further inspire your lives for good.

We have a beautiful world and together there is nothing stopping us from making it a good experience for everyone.

WEDNESDAY, SEPTEMBER 16, 2009

Gratitude for Bella

Today, Brian's widow, Anna, welcomed their much-anticipated second daughter, Bella Aspen Cardall. She came from God's arms and Brian's to his eternal love, Anna.

While I sit in my room recovering from this miraculously orchestrated heart transplant, I'm humbled and grateful at the very thought of life. We come and go. It is so fragile, so delicate, so priceless, and so incredible. And I thank God for orchestrating our lives and teaching my family the joy in the journey.

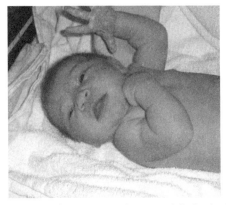

Bella Aspen Cardall, daughter of Brian and Anna Cardall, shortly after her birth.

THURSDAY, SEPTEMBER 17, 2009

Fitted for a Better World

Today I walked for thirty minutes without oxygen and nearly tube free (with the exception of my chest tubes that are draining fluid), from my room at Primary Children's Medical Center over the long hallway to the University of Utah Hospital. And although I have to gown up and wear a mask and gloves to protect myself from infection, I have never felt so alive!

I should be home soon, but I'll be back every other day for the usual poking and prodding, biopsies, and rehab typical of a post-transplant life. Eventually, I'll have a stabilized drug regimen and be on my way to an almost normal life with a new transplanted organ.

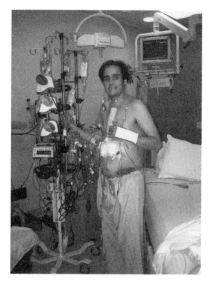

*As part of the recovery process, I went on walks
taking all of my tubes and pumps with me.*

And what to do now?

Over the next couple of weeks, I plan to wrap up this
blog for a season in order to focus all my time and attention on my wife and my little girl. I think I'll have Eden take
me shopping for a bicycle. I'm sure she'll have a good idea.
Maybe she'll help me buy me some tap shoes so I can dance
with her.

This blog, *Living for Eden,* will remain online and available as a resource for the folks Googling medical information
and looking for personal help.

The road has been long and difficult. We have experienced every kind of emotion. There have been deep discussions in the darkest hours of evenings concerning the "what ifs." How would my family live without a father and husband? Such questions are sobering. Many tears have flowed. We've spent countless hours on our knees seeking help. And the help came through the arms of those who love people and love God. I have learned a great deal about the character of my community. There is more virtue and good in the world than evil. People quietly go about doing good, and I'm moved to follow in their footsteps.

I've shared insights and probably preached principles. I know that we cannot learn joy in this world without experiencing the challenges of life. Through our suffering we gain important virtues: wisdom, compassion, love, charity, hope, faith, sacrifice, and many more.

Neal A. Maxwell stated, "We have a Father who loves us specifically and gives us things to do and, because he loves us, will cause us, at times, to have our souls stretched and to be fitted for a better world by coping with life in this world."[2]

This experience has transformed me. I would not trade this past year for all the wealth or power in the world. But, of course, if I had all that I would have the ability to shout from the rooftops an eternal law from the New Testament which most people can agree with: "Love the Lord thy God with all thy heart, and with all thy soul, and with all thy strength, and with all thy mind; and thy neighbour as thyself" (Luke 10:27). And also a powerful statement in the book of

Ephesians, which can help most marriages, "Husbands, love your wives, even as Christ also loved the church, and gave himself for it" (Ephesians 5:25).

MONDAY, SEPTEMBER 21, 2009
Look, Mom, I'm a Real Boy

Doctors completed a full heart biopsy this afternoon. My new heart is beautiful! I have some minor rejection factors and pressure, but that can be resolved by the proper chemistry of drugs. All people with transplants have a low immune system because the new heart or organ is not the body's own DNA and the body wants to fight it like a virus. This is why people with transplants take a range of drugs such as Prograf, Cellcept, Septra, Valcyte, and Prednisone. It's all a matter of chemistry and taking medication on time to help resolve issues and protect the new organ from rejection and failure.

Unfortunately, because of my poor immune system and the fact that we are approaching the season for flu, swine flu, colds, and more, it will be some time before I am able to go out into public places, which may be difficult for someone like me who enjoys people.

My kidneys and other organs are functioning beautifully. We worried about future issues with my organs because of the protein-losing enteropathy, but that is working itself out. The varicose veins in my legs have disappeared, as well as some spider veins. My skin and color look normal. My eyes are clear and blue. My daughter thinks I'm wearing new lipstick. The remarkable human heart works miracles in and of itself. I'm amazed and humbled!

For the past five years, I've worn oxygen at night to help me sleep. We've had a concentrator in our home with a fifty-foot cord. Eden always followed the cord if she wanted to find her dad. In addition, I had a fanny pack carrying the medication Milrinone, which flowed through a PICC line into my heart for almost ten months. Of course, the home-health care company put its logo right on front of the fanny pack, so I felt like I walked around plugging the company. My brother-in-law thought I should have imprinted paulcardall.com on the bag instead.

I've been looking forward to this—to doctors removing all of the chest tubes and IVs from my body. I'm able to walk around and enjoy the world without any tubes or other attachments. It made me think of a very old Disney song about not having any strings to hold me down.

THURSDAY, SEPTEMBER 24, 2009

Home Is Where the Heart Is

Leaving through the hospital doors with my arm around Lynnette was breathtaking. Was I anxious to get home? I still don't know. *Shocked* is the word I might use. I could not believe I was going home.

Primary Children's Medical Center had become my

home and family. Leaving them behind, I felt some interesting emotions. Of course, patients continue to cycle through their care. Whatever joyous celebration we experienced in my recovery, the nurses caring for me signed off their responsibility and went back to work caring for the many sick children still fighting for their lives. And yet there is not much public recognition for these quiet and faithful employees who bless so many lives.

After picking Eden up from a cousin's home, we drove up our street. Loads of pink and red heart-shaped balloons had been placed all over our front yard, by my sister Carol I later found out. I was proud to know our neighbors knew this was a great day in our lives.

Our neighbors had mowed the lawn and trimmed everything. They even picked the tomatoes they had planted in a garden they helped create many months ago. I had told Lynnette I was looking forward to eating those tomatoes, not knowing if that would really happen. I expected to be home shortly before Thanksgiving or Christmas. My anatomy and recovery have been beyond anyone's true comprehension. And we had planned for the worst while trusting in God and His ability to orchestrate the events of our lives.

Walking through our front door I was overwhelmed with gratitude and humility at our many blessings. The support and love of people who've bought my CDs is sobering. We have a quiet home on a peaceful street. Peace fills the walls. I attribute this to Lynnette and her divine nature. I was reminded of these words by religious leader Harold B. Lee,

"The most important part of the Lord's work you will ever do will be within the walls of your own home."[3]

Spending a quiet evening at home with Eden and Lynnette was something special and nostalgic. I think Eden went through four or five outfits until we were able to get her off to a ballet/tap dance class in her cute pink tutu. Of course, she kept touching my chest to feel my heart. And from time to time she'd say with a tender, sweet smile, "Dad, hold my hand."

Now more than ever I know home is where the heart is. And with tears of gratitude in my heart I know I'm home to stay.

✺ *Chapter 30* ✺

"PAUL CARDALL RECOVERY A 'MIRACLE'"

BY CARRIE A. MOORE

DESERET NEWS

Wednesday, Sept. 23, 2009

Heart recipient comes home far earlier than doctors had expected.

As pink and red heart-shaped balloons bob in the breeze outside their home, Paul and Lynnette Cardall are examining prescription bottles inside.

There's a new heart beating in Paul's chest. Lynnette's heart, for the first time in more than a year, is finally beginning to rest easy.

The LDS musician and his wife came home from the hospital on Wednesday, weeks before anyone had believed would be possible after Paul's heart transplant two weeks ago at Primary Children's Medical Center.

Doctors had told them it would be five to six weeks before he would be strong enough to unplug all the oxygen and IV lines so he could walk away a free man, but as he has done so many times before, Cardall surprised them all.

Before his recent surgery, the 36-year-old husband and father was the oldest Utah patient with his specific type of congenital heart disease to have survived to his age without a transplant. To have him home so soon, and without experiencing any major complications, "is a dream come true. It's just a miracle," Lynnette Cardall said.

Before leaving the hospital, the couple was shown Cardall's old heart, "a football-sized" organ he said he had been lucky to live so long with, considering it was only about half-functional. He said that as he held a portion of it in his hands, turning it over and over and examining the stitches from past surgeries, that was the moment when he "truly understood that somebody else is clearly in charge of our lives."

Future medical students at the University of Utah will hold his old heart in their hands also as a learning tool to help understand congenital heart disease, even as Cardall continues on a series of anti-rejection drugs to keep his body from rejecting the new organ. . . .

When the new heart was placed inside his chest on the operating table, the surgeon turned around for a moment to grab the paddles that would send an electric current through the heart so it would start beating again.

"He looked back and the heart had started beating on its own, just like it was meant to be there," Cardall said. His year-long journey to a transplant, after he was listed for a heart in August 2008 through the surgery and recovery itself, has been "sobering, miraculous and divinely orchestrated," he said Wednesday, standing in his kitchen next to a cache of pill bottles as if he were just preparing to fix dinner.

The normalcy of life without oxygen tanks, constant fatigue and the continuous "what if" thoughts has yet to really sink in, but the Cardall family is more than ready to let that happen. Three-year-old Eden has seemed to take it all in stride, back from her tap dance lesson in a pink tutu and blithely oblivious to the life-or-death drama that her dad's most recent hospital stay entailed.

Cardall will return to see his doctors often as they monitor his daily intake of medication via computer, including at least five anti-rejections drugs.

He's set a text message on his iPhone to be sent 15 minutes before he is scheduled to take each of at least a dozen different medications.

It will take time for his sternum to heal and his immune system to rebound, so he'll be spending a lot of time at home with family. He looks forward to the rehab program doctors will implement to help him rebuild muscle lost as his body grew steadily weaker before and after surgery.

He's also anxious to "be athletic" with activities like running and hiking that haven't been possible for years, and he looks forward to a stay in the family cabin in the coming weeks without the altitude sickness he used to experience there. Skiing is a goal he's set for next spring, with a climb to the top of Mount Olympus scheduled for summer, in commemoration of his late brother Brian's life.

As for his music, Cardall said he's ready to work on some things at home, but he won't be performing publicly until a February concert dubbed "Living for Eden," part two, named after a recent album he released in honor of his daughter. Last spring, fellow LDS musicians put on a benefit concert by the same name, donating the proceeds to the Cardall family for medical expenses.

He now plans to do the same for others who are dealing with large medical bills caused by congenital heart disease.

He'll also be making the final posts to his transplant blog in the next week or two, though the contents will still be available online for anyone looking for information about congenital heart disease and his experience with the journey to—and through—surgery.

As an initial nod to what he expects will be a new lease on a life of more normalcy, Cardall said one of his first acts on arriving home was to "eat a plate full of tomatoes," after neighbors came Tuesday night to clean up his yard and harvest the tomato plants they placed there last spring.

Despite the gravity of his illness, they planted with the hope that he would be around to at least see the fall harvest.

So when they see him walking the neighborhood soon, it's certain they won't be disappointed.[1]

Chapter 31

LIVING FOR EDEN

PART 16

SATURDAY, SEPTEMBER 26, 2009

Freedom

This evening, for the first time in almost a year, I took a shower free of any tubes connected to me. I felt so peaceful and free.

FRIDAY, OCTOBER 2, 2009

"Love Is on the Move"

Last Sunday, after I'd been home from the hospital for four days, our neighbor dropped off her new convertible BMW. She said, "Here you go. It's yours for two days." As I've always said, "It's better to be trusted than to be loved." Of course, we put the top down on the car. In the back of the vehicle, Eden was snug in her car seat with a cute jacket.

With the wind blowing through our hair, Lynnette drove us up the nearest canyon by our home. The trees in Little Cottonwood Canyon were changing color. The once-green leaves were beautiful red, orange, and yellow.

We pumped up the volume as we listened to a favorite band called Leeland. As they sang, "Love Is on the Move," we headed up to Alta ski resort, where we parked our neighbor's car.

For the first time in twenty-two years, I felt no altitude sickness, which I often had up in the mountains because of my old heart's anatomy and the Fontan procedure. We walked some distance up a small trail off the side of the road. I felt amazing.

Driving home, all we could do is cry because of what God has done for our little family. Hundreds of people have prayed. Little children have pleaded with God for Eden's daddy. Surely the Creator orchestrated something beautiful, and I hope others may feel our same joy.

I feel endurance, and I recognize blood flowing through my body. Like slowly dipping the tips of your fingers in warm water, I can now feel a sensation in my fingers. I'm composing music with more feeling. My nails grow. I used to have to clip my nails every other month. Now, it's every week. I don't get winded or light-headed talking. I can follow Eden around the block as she rides her bike and still feel like going another mile. My appetite is strong. I'm up early walking as the sun rises. Needless to say, I feel alive and vibrant. Is this

Eden took this photo of Lynnette and me on my first hike up the mountains.
She somehow managed to capture the shape of a heart between us.

what it feels like to be normal? If so, count your blessings.
You all have been greatly blessed by the Creator.

I had a chance to see and hold my old heart in the lab
prior to leaving the hospital. Some of the heart had gone to
another lab, and a small part of the left atrium and superior
vena cava is still in me. What I held in my hands looked
awful and somewhat disgusting. Pacemaker leads were still
in the fatty substance on the outer walls. Stitches from previous surgeries were still in place in various locations. My
right atrium looked like a four- to five-inch balloon with very
thin walls. It had been deflated. That's how Dr. Kaza was
able to remove the heart. The left ventricle and left atrium
were covered with a thick, fatty wall. I saw my mitral valve,
which struggled to pump oxygenated blood through my body

for thirty-six years. As I held this heavy, oversized heart in both hands, I said to the pathologist, "How in the world did I survive all these years on this thing?"

He replied with a puzzled smile, "That's what we're trying to figure out."

At that moment, for the first time, I saw beyond my faith or spiritual hope of a Creator or God. I held the physical evidence in my hands. Clearly, someone else is breathing life into our bodies. Experts wonder how this pump sustained my life for thirty-six years, struggling to push blood through my body. But the surgeons figured a way out. They made it work.

I asked a friend who is a cardiac anesthesiologist about challenging surgeries and the delicate matters of life and death. Why are some taken home to God? Why do some stay? He said, "Sometimes, no matter how hard we work and no matter if we are doing everything correctly, the patient for some strange reason passes away. And then there are times where we think to ourselves 'there is no way this person is going to survive.' But we go ahead and do the best job we can and the person lives. It's hard to understand such circumstances. Obviously, someone else is running the show."

Because of His tender mercies, our Heavenly Father has preserved my life all of these years. And now I have a new heart. I am greatly blessed. I don't know why. I'm humbled by the miracle that was beautifully orchestrated over the last year. All I know is that God Almighty has breathed life back into my body. He is my Friend, your Friend, my Father in Heaven, and your Father in Heaven. He is real. He lives.

And like the scars in the palm of Jesus' hands, I have scars to remind me of His love, mercy, and grace.

My soul has been stretched. I will continue to search and seek out soul-stretching experiences, because in this I find joy, wisdom, happiness, and a personal relationship with God. His purpose and plan for each person is real. There is life after death. I do not doubt. We will see our loved ones who've passed away. I will enjoy a reunion with my brother. Until then, may we all enjoy our life and find joy in the journey.

WEDNESDAY, OCTOBER 21, 2009
A Bike and Answers to Prayer

In one of the last e-mails I received from my brother Brian he wrote, "I am excited to see what you accomplish with 100 percent capacity post transplant! Maybe we should get you a road bike or some skis or something."

In the pediatric intensive care unit (PICU), as I recovered from surgery, I noticed I had never felt so alive. Blood was flowing through my body, and I could feel it giving new life and energy to my soul. With an ambitious spirit, I said to my wife, "I am going to get a bike and ride around like a crazy little kid." Doctors advised me to wait six to eight weeks for my sternum to heal.

I was anxious to buy a bike, but my family kept telling me not to go out and buy one yet, because my sister-in-law

Enjoying a bike ride with my daughter, Eden, on a quiet evening.

Anna had a connection with one of the local bicycle shops. She and I spoke over the phone, and I mentioned to her what Brian had said to me in one of his last e-mails. She said, "I know just what you need and what Brian would have gotten for you." I trusted her instincts.

As I anxiously awaited word, I set aside some money I had been saving to help pay for my new joyride.

The other night, my family gathered at my parents' home. It was a beautiful evening with the leaves changing colors. My mom suggested that we go outside while the weather was still nice. I replied that I would come outside in a few minutes, as soon as I finished transferring some video my dad had taken of Eden and me up the canyon.

I walked outside to find everyone smiling. I looked toward them and saw a beautiful black road bike leaning up against a chair by where my sister-in-law Anna was standing. She had found me a bike, and this was not your average bike.

I was so excited that I could barely contain myself. Then, Anna said, "It's Brian's bike. He used to ride this thing around like a silly little boy, going off jumps." My heart was overwhelmed with emotion. I had no idea my brother had a bike. He never told me about it, and there are no photos of him riding it. Overcome with joy, I asked, "What do I owe you for this?" She answered, "I'm not going to sell you Brian's bike. It's yours. He wants you to have it." Thank you, Anna.

We all miss my brother. Now that I'm recovering and feel more alive, I think about Brian's death each day. I remember sobbing like a child over his casket with oxygen tubes in my nose. Many of my tears are buried with him.

Since his tragic death, I have asked our Heavenly Father in humble prayer, "Why Brian? Why not me? I'm the sick one. He's thriving. He's amazing. He had plenty of time to do many, many great things." I carried this with me until the day I received word that a heart had become available.

In the quiet moment of night, prior to my surgery, came the tender impression from our Father in Heaven, which said to me, "I need him." Comfort filled the room and I felt a powerful sense of peace and solace. My old heart burned and felt empowered. Then, I felt another impression say to me, "I need you here."

I have no doubt, when all is said and done, and I'm finished with what I want to do here, that I will join my brother in the afterlife.

Each of us, you and me, has a purpose or destiny. You have talents, gifts, and a personality that can enable you to accomplish a lot of good in this world and in the next. We have within us the love, service, and selfless acts of kindness needed to strengthen our marriages, families, community, and the world.

I know Brian is doing special things. I'm sure he finds time to ride a bike, climb mountains, reunite with family members who have passed on, observe the stunning new colors of the flowers and nature, and ask a lot of questions.

I believe my brother has been with God, felt of His comforting embrace, and heard the song of redeeming love. I believe this is the same for the millions upon millions.

I realize these thoughts and answers are deep or heavy. Where do I get this information and confidence? In the Book of Mormon: Another Testament of Jesus Christ, we find this comforting answer: "Behold, it has been made known unto me [a prophet named Alma] by an angel, that the spirits of all men, as soon as they are departed from this mortal body, yea, the spirits of all men, whether they be good or evil, are taken home to that God who gave them life. And then shall it come to pass, that the spirits of those who are righteous are received into a state of happiness, which is called paradise, a state of rest, a state of peace, where they shall rest from all their troubles and from all care, and sorrow" (Alma 40:11–12).

Every time I get on Brian's bike and ride around like a kid, I'll be reminded of my relationship with him. It will last beyond this world because life is eternal. That life is made possible by Jesus Christ, the Creator of this earth. Coming to earth is part of a great plan. We are here to get a body, learn how to control it, overcome addictions, and return home to the God who gave us life. There, I believe, we will continue to assist the millions of our brothers and sisters who are struggling to find their way back home.

As I regain my strength, I will try to continue to do here what I believe Brian is doing in a world of spirits, which is offering hope to people.

What do people need? They need kindness. They need to know they are not alone. They need to know there are those who love them. They need to know in their hearts that our Heavenly Father, the Supreme Being, knows their names and that they can talk to Him in a prayer by themselves in a quiet place. They need to know, as I do, that He will listen.

When I am at home with my daughter and she's in another room with her eyes closed, she can't see me, but she knows I'm there.

As the saying goes, "A man never stands taller than when he is on his knees." As we kneel in prayer, we can seek and find help, strength, and answers to life's most challenging questions.

To my dear brother Brian and his beautiful wife Anna, their new baby Bella Aspen and their toddler Ava Sky, thank you for the bike! I'll ride it like a silly boy.

TUESDAY, OCTOBER 27, 2009

Being There for Others

Each week as I attend my transplant clinic at Primary Children's Medical Center in Salt Lake City I run into other families who have a child who has a heart defect or is waiting for a heart transplant.

This past week I was fortunate to spend a brief moment with Lucas and his mother. They checked into the hospital in the room next to me shortly before I left home. Lucas needs a heart soon. He is a sweet infant with a beautiful smile who gets the affection of the nurses who cared for me.

In Lucas's room I could feel God's love, and I know He is deeply involved in their battle. I was honored to be in the presence of Lucas.

As I was leaving the hospital on the elevator after visiting with Lucas I accidentally got off on the wrong floor. These things are not a coincidence because I was fortunate to run into Briton and his mother, Stacee.

I was wearing my green mask since I was in a public environment, which protects me from catching the flu or a cold. Unfortunately, my mask frightened young Briton. I felt bad and offered him my Three Musketeer candy bar I had just purchased. I had a good time talking to them and I know God is deeply involved in their lives.

Briton received the Fontan procedure several weeks ago and is doing quite well. He should have a long life ahead of him. The Fontan has greatly improved from the time I received it more than twenty years ago.

As I visited with these two families I again realized that even though I feel a season of victory there are others in the midst of a hard battle.

Often, so many of us are oblivious to what's happening next door or in our own homes.

I hope I never forget or lose sight of the fact that there are children and adults throughout the world in need of our kindness, love, prayers, and a little help.

My scars are reminders.

You and I can only do so much. We can improve the world by choosing to mourn with those that mourn and comfort those who stand in need of comfort.

I believe God will guide us to where we need to be to serve others.

If I've learned anything at all through my experiences it is that I know God is the Father of us all. He loves his children more than we can imagine. We can trust Him.

No matter how much we do or try to do to help, in the end it's the love of God that is going to help ease the pain and suffering of others. I felt His love through the kind acts of others.

Of course we need seasons to celebrate!

However, I've learned that even though we are in a state of celebration or like we don't have a care in the world, we should have within each of us the strength to listen to our impressions and be ready to go and do all that is asked of us.

So what can we do today?

Instead of focusing on everyone we know with a trial, try selecting one person in need and go and do something about it. Maybe that means offering up a prayer, sending a thoughtful e-mail, making a phone call, delivering a kind note, or simply listening to their burdens without saying much. Be a listening ear, and enjoy the time you have with that person.

By doing this you'll find more peace and happiness because you're thinking of others.

LOOKING BACK

A month or two after I was listed for a heart transplant, my parents, brothers, and sisters, along with their spouses—a few of whom were in town from Dallas and Las Vegas—gathered in my grandparents' home to discuss the transplant list and the serious nature of my heart failure. We had a family prayer and then my Dad said something to the effect, "We are going to have a rather tough year ahead of us, but I feel Paul is going to make it."

After we discussed several other issues, my father and brothers gathered around me and blessed me according to the traditions of my Mormon faith. Led by my father and with the faith of my sisters in the room, my brothers gave me what we call a priesthood blessing. As part of the experience I was told I would feel God's love through the ordeal and be blessed with strength to endure the challenges ahead. In addition, my father was impressed to say I would get well.

Looking back now, who would have thought that two of

the men in that room would have passed away leaving me with a miraculous recovery and a second chance at life?

Within seven months, my younger brother Brian was tragically killed in a Taser incident, the details of which are confusing, ridiculous, and painful. This was a sad and unfortunate event that obviously could have been prevented. I continue to wrestle with the nature of his death.

Here I was waiting for a new heart, which requires someone to die, my whole family praying for my survival, and another member of our family dies.

Could life be any more ironic? Where could I find understanding and peace? How can any of us find answers to life's most challenging moments with such tragedy?

Devastated and heartbroken, our family understood the sacrifice, heartache, and pain my donor's family would feel losing their son, brother, father, and friend.

In addition, my grandfather Layton quietly slipped to the other side on a Sunday evening in November 2009. This was a much more welcomed occasion because he had enjoyed a full life and raised a large posterity of more than one hundred people loyal to one another.

For me, with the passing of these great men, including my donor, I found strength in prayer, attending Church to be with others who also love God, reading inspiring books, and overall, listening intently to music. The right type of music always opens a conduit to heaven for me.

I was particularly inspired by fellow musician Steven Curtis Chapman, who released an album inspired by his struggle to deal with the death of his own daughter. His son backed the car out of the driveway, accidentally injuring the little girl, who was later pronounced dead at the hospital.

Truly, this has been a period of life and death, joy and sadness, miracles and tragedy. I have been grieving not only my brother and grandfather, but I am grieving for my donor. Nonetheless, I do believe out of these ashes beauty will rise!

As I've taken this journey I've come to know other people suffering from congenital heart defects and terminal diseases. I've attended many funerals. Each one has been extremely special and important and has reaffirmed to me the reality of God and life after death. To say this life is all there is, for me, is madness. No matter what science proves, science belongs to God. It is His tool to save mankind and redeem them from a fallen state to a state of eternal happiness.

I am grateful for life. We have no idea when it will be over. We don't know our time to leave this beautiful world unless we have a terminal diagnosis. As one who was faced with death in 2009, and somehow by the grace of God has been given a new lease on life, I can't tell you how thankful I am for those of you who prayed selflessly for our family this past year. Truly, 2009 has been one to remember. Our souls have been stretched and our relationship to the Creator has been strengthened.

For more information on congenital heart disease and other related issues, visit www.paulcardall.com.

April 24, 1973: Potts-Smith Shunt

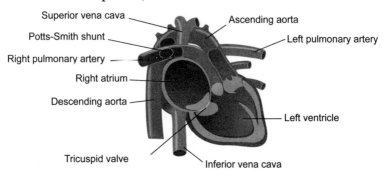

Diagnoses: Double-inlet single ventricle, subvalvar and valvar pulmonary stenosis (functional atresia), atrial septal defect, right aortic arch, patent ductus arteriosus

Surgical Procedure: Potts-Smith shunt: anastomosis of the descending aorta to the right pulmonary artery. Performed at 22 hours old on April 26, 1973.

December 6, 1986: Saphenous Vein Graft

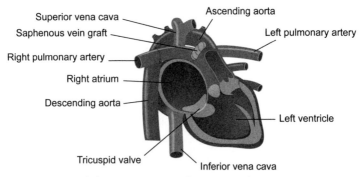

Diagnoses: Staphylococcus aureus endarteritis resulting in a mycotic aneurysm of the right pulmonary artery adjacent to the Potts-Smith anastomosis.

Surgical Procedure: Takedown of the Potts-Smith anastomosis, resection of the right-pulmonary artery and placement of a 6 mm spiral saphenous vein graft from the aortic arch to the main pulmonary artery (vein taken from left leg).

August 14, 1987: The Fontan

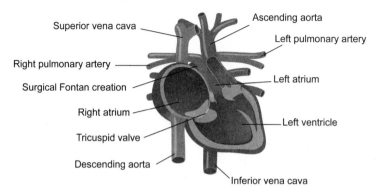

Fontan procedure: Creation of a 21 mm anastomosis of the right atrium to the pulmonary artery, takedown of the saphenous vein graft/shunt, ligation of a patent ductus arteriosus, closure of the right atrioventricular valve with a patch of Dacron and closure of the atrial septal defect leaving the coronary sinus to drain into the left artrium. Placement of an AV sequential pacing system.

Various revisions of pacing system: performed on August 26, 1987; April 27, 1994; May 5, 1997; October 23, 2000; October 1, 2002. Incisional atrial re-entry tachycardia and atrial fibrillation requiring cardio version.

A Normal Heart

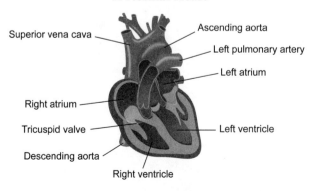

ENDNOTES

Chapter 1

1. Cecil Frances Alexander, "There Is a Green Hill Far Away," *Hymns of the Church of Jesus Christ of Latter-day Saints* (Salt Lake City: The Church of Jesus Christ of Latter-day Saints, 1985), no. 194.

Chapter 3

1. Dieter F. Uchtdorf, "The Infinite Power of Hope," *Ensign,* November 2008, 21.

Chapter 4

1. *U.S. News and World Report,* November 11, 2000. Article quoted the results of a study in Rodney Stark, "The Rise of a New World Faith," *Review of Religious Research* 26 (September 1984), 18–27.

2. Doug Robinson, "Reporter's Beat Was LDS Leaders," *Deseret News,* March 27, 2006. © 2006 *Deseret News,* Salt Lake City. Used by permission.

Chapter 8

1. John F. Kennedy, http://thinkexist.com/quotation/the_problems_of_the_world_cannot_possibly_be/212265.html

2. Theodor Billroth, quoted in Alan S. Coulson and Michael E. Hanlon, "War and the First Century of Heart Surgery," *Relevance* (The Quarterly Journal of the Great War Society), 1 (Winter 1997), 377. http://worldwar1. com/tgws/rel009.htm, accessed June 7, 2010.

3. Stephen Paget, quoted in James G. Chandler and Stephen E. Novak, "Cardiac Surgery's Insurgent Evolution," *John James Surgical Society,* 12 (Spring 2009), 3. http://www.columbiasurgery.org/news/john/jjss_sp09.pdf

4. John A. Waldhausen, "The Early History of Congenital Heart Surgery: Closed Heart Operations," *The Annals of Thoracic Surgery,* 64 (1997), 1553–39. http://ats.ctsnetjournals.org/cgi/content/full/64/5/1533, accessed June 7, 2010.

Chapter 13

1. Jerry Seinfield, http://www.oprah.com/omagazine/Oprah-Interviews-Jerry-Seinfield/7

2. Dieter F. Uchtdorf, "The Infinite Power of Hope," *Ensign,* November 2008, 22.

3. Russell M. Nelson, *From Heart to Heart* (Salt Lake City: Quality Press, 1979), 287–88.

4. Uchtdorf, "Power of Hope," 24.

5. Gordon B. Hinckley, from a conversation with Bob Pickles, witnessed by Duane Cardall.

6. C. S. Lewis, *The Problem of Pain* (New York: HarperCollins, 2001), 91.

7. From the movie *Braveheart* (1995), http://en.wikiquote.org/wiki/Braveheart

8. Albert Einstein, http://en.wikiquote.org/wiki/Albert_Einstein

9. Mahatma Gandhi, http://thinkexist.com/quotation/the_best_way_to_find_yourself_is_to_lose_yourself/148517.html

10. Gordon B. Hinckley, "Taking the Gospel to Britain," *Ensign,* July 1987, 7.

11. Neal A. Maxwell, "It's Service, Not Status, That Counts," *Ensign,* July 1975, 7.

Chapter 14

1. Carrie A. Moore, "Pianist's Competitors Rally for Fellow Artist," *Deseret News,* April 11, 2009. © 2009 *Deseret News,* Salt Lake City. Used by permission.

Chapter 15

1. Neal A. Maxwell, "Irony: The Crust on the Bread of Adversity," *Ensign,* May 1989, 6-3.

2. Joseph Smith, *Teachings of the Prophet Joseph Smith,* comp. Joseph Fielding Smith, (Salt Lake City: Deseret Book, 1938), 304.

3. Albert Einstein, http://thinkexist.com/quotation/in_the_middle_of_difficulty_lies_opportunity/10122.html

4. Thomas S. Monson, "Finding Joy in the Journey," *Ensign,* November 2008, 85.

5. Abraham Lincoln, http://www.goodreads.com/quotes/show/18542

Chapter 16

1. Stephen Ambrose, as quoted in Harriet Rubin, "Past Track to the Future," (April 30, 2001), http://www.fastcompany.com/magazine/46/ambrose.html, accessed June 7, 2010.

2. *Church History in the Fulness of Times* (Salt Lake City: The Church of Jesus Christ of Latter-day Saints, 2003), 175.

3. Charles Richard Snelgrove and Emily Brooksbank Snelgrove, Their Ancestry, Life, and Descendents, Emily Elizabeth Snelgrove

Davey and Irene Mercedese Snelgrove Higgins, comps. (Bountiful, UT: Family History Publishers, 1990), 18.

4. Ibid.

5. Charles Dickens, "The Uncommercial Traveller," *All the Year Round* 9, 4 July 1963, 444, 446, http://www.online-literature.com/dickens/uncommercial-traveller/22/

6. Ibid.

7. Snelgrove, 21.

8. Ibid.

Chapter 17

1. Neal A. Maxwell, *". . . A More Excellent Way"* (Salt Lake City: Deseret Book, 1967), 89.

2. Neal A. Maxwell, *Of One Heart* (Salt Lake City: Deseret Book Co., 1975), 14.

3. Martin Luther King, Jr., *Martin Luther King, Jr.: We Shall Overcome* (audiobook), Speechworks (August 2000).

4. Leo Tolstoy, http://thinkexist.com/quotation/the_two_most_powerful_warriors_are_patience_and/214096.html

5. Stephen Ambrose, *Band of Brothers: E Company, 506th Regiment, 101st Airborne from Normandy to Hitler's Eagle's Nest* (New York City: Simon & Schuster, 1992), 95–96.

6. C. S. Lewis, http://www.quotationspage.com/quote/37800.html

7. *Teachings of Presidents of the Church: David O. McKay* (Salt Lake City: The Church of Jesus Christ of Latter-day Saints, 2003), 182, emphasis in original.

8. Maya Angelou, "Laugh and Dare to Love," an interview by Linda Wolf, in *Generation NExT,* Winter 1995–96, 45).

9. Neal A. Maxwell, "'Endure It Well,'" *Ensign,* May 1990, 33.

Chapter 18

1. John Hollenhorst, "Son of KSL Editorial Director Dies after Being Tased by Police," KDS News Reporting, June 9, 2009. Used by permission.

Chapter 20

1. Rita S. Robinson, "Saturday," *Children's Songbook* (Salt Lake City: The Church of Jesus Christ of Latter-day Saints, 2000), 196.

Chapter 22

1. Stuart K Hine, "How Great Thou Art," *Hymns of the Church of Jesus Christ of Latter-day Saints* (Salt Lake City: The Church of Jesus Christ of Latter-day Saints, 1985). No. 86. Used by permission of Hope Publishing Company.

Chapter 24

1. Stephen M. Shuster, "A Trained Scientist," given at the funeral services for Brian Cardall. In author's possession. Used by permission.

Chapter 25

1. "Bring the Rain," written by Bart Millard, Jim Bryson, Nathan Cochran, Barry Graul, Mike Scheuchzer, and Robby Shaffer. © 2006 Simpleville Music and Wet as a Fish Music (ASCAP). All rights administered by Simpleville Music, Inc. Used by permission.

2. Rudyard Kipling, "My Boy Jack," *Twenty Poems from Rudyard Kipling* (London: Methuen, 1918). See also http://en.wikipedia.org/wiki/My_Boy_Jack_(poem)

3. This quote has been attributed to Edward Erwin, a minister of the First Baptist Church of Kentucky.

4. Thomas S. Monson, "Looking Back and Moving Forward," *Ensign,* May 2008, 90.

5. Sanskrit proverb, http://thinkexist.com/quotation/yesterday_is_but_a_dream-tomorrow_but_a_vision/8324.html

6. Aristotle, http://www.quotationspage.com/quote/37270.html

7. Helen Keller, http://www.quotationspage.com/quote/30187.html

8. Aldous Huxley, *Texts and Pretexts: An Anthology of Commentaries* (London: Chatto and Windus, 1932).

9. Thomas S. Monson, "In Quest of the Abundant Life," *Ensign,* March 1988, 2.

10. Henry David Thoreau, *Simplify, Simplify and Other Quotations by Henry David Thoreau* (New York: Columbia University Press, 1996).

11. Jeffrey R. Holland, "The Message: How Do I Love Thee?" *New Era,* October 2003, 6.

12. L. Tom Perry, "The Importance of the Family," *Ensign,* May 2003, 40.

13. Neal A. Maxwell, "But for A Small Moment," address given 1 September 1974 at Brigham Young University, in *Brigham Young University 1974 Speeches* (Provo, UT: Brigham Young University, 1975). Also found at http://speeches.byu.edu/reader/reader.php?id=6066.

14. Richard Paul Evans, as recorded by author on a book tour.

15. Maxwell, "But for a Small Moment."

16. "I Will Not Be Still," written by Tyler Castleton, Staci Peters, and Greg Simpson. © 1999 *Diamond* Aire Music (ASCAP) / Fog Dog Music (ASCAP) / Paulista Music Publishing (ASCAP). Used by permission.

17. Winston Churchill, http://www.brainyquote.com/quotes/quotes/w/winstonchu103788.html

18. Duke Ellington, http://thinkexist.com/quotation/a_problem_is_a_chance_for_you_to_do_your_best/13194.html

Chapter 28

1. Carrie A. Moore, "With a New Heart Beating in His Chest, Paul Cardall Beats Odds Yet Again," *Deseret News,* September 10, 2009. © 2009 *Deseret News,* Salt Lake City. Used by permission.

Chapter 29

1. Neal A. Maxwell, address given 24 May 1999 at funeral services for Lynne Sanders Nelson, mother of cellist Steven Sharp Nelson; transcript in author's possession.

2. Neal A. Maxwell, "But for A Small Moment," address given 1 September 1974 at Brigham Young University, in *Brigham Young University 1974 Speeches* (Provo, UT: Brigham Young University, 1975). Also found at http://speeches.byu.edu/reader/reader. php?id=6066.

3. Harold B. Lee, *The Teachings of Harold B. Lee,* ed. Clyde J. Williams (Salt Lake City: Bookcraft, 1996), 280.

Chapter 30

1. Carrie A. Moore, "Paul Cardall Recovery a 'Miracle,'" *Deseret News,* September 23, 2009. © 2009 *Deseret News,* Salt Lake City. Used by permission.

PHOTO AND ILLUSTRATION CREDITS

INDEX